Hey, Coach!

Positive Differences You Can Make for Young People in Sports

An asset-builder's guide to common coaching situations

by Neal Starkman

Hey, Coach!
Positive Differences You Can Make for Young People in Sports
Neal Starkman

At the time of publication, all facts and figures cited herein are the most current available; all telephone numbers, addresses, and Web site URLs are accurate and active; all publications, organizations, Web sites, and other resources exist as described in this book; and all efforts have been made to verify them. The author and Search Institute make no warranty or guarantee concerning the information and materials given out by organizations or content found at Web sites that are cited herein, and we are not responsible for any changes that occur after this book's publication. If you find an error or believe that a resource listed herein is not as described, please contact Client Services at Search Institute.

10 9 8 7 6 5 4 3 2 1
Printed on acid-free paper in the United States of America.

Search Institute
615 First Avenue Northeast, Suite 125
Minneapolis, MN 55413
www.search-institute.org
612-376-8955 • 800-888-7828

Credits
Editors: Rebecca Aldridge, Kathryn (Kay) L. Hong
Book Design: Percolator
Production Coordinator: Mary Ellen Buscher

Library of Congress Cataloging-in-Publication Data
Starkman, Neal.
Hey, coach! : positive differences you can make for young people in sports / by Neal Starkman.
p. cm.
Includes bibliographical references.
ISBN 1-57482-832-0 (paperbook : alk. paper)
1. Sports for children--Coaching. 2. Coaches (Athletics)--Conduct of life. I. Title.
GV709.24.S83 2004
796'.07'7--dc22 2004010988

About Search Institute
Search Institute is an independent, nonprofit, nonsectarian organization whose mission is to provide leadership, knowledge, and resources to promote healthy children, youth, and communities. The institute collaborates with others to promote long-term organizational and cultural change that supports its mission. For a free information packet, call 800-888-7828.

About This Resource
Search Institute's Healthy Communities • Healthy Youth® initiative seeks to unite individuals, organizations, and their leaders to join together in nurturing competent, caring, and responsible children and adolescents. Major support for Search Institute's Healthy Communities • Healthy Youth (HC • HY) initiative is provided by Thrivent Financial for Lutherans. Lutheran Brotherhood, now Thrivent Financial for Lutherans, is the founding national sponsor for HC • HY.

CONTENTS

ACKNOWLEDGMENTS

Thank you to Search Institute's Becky Aldridge for her valuable editing and Nancy Tellett-Royce for her timely references.

Thank you to Anna Rabel and Brad McClure of Seattle's Washington Middle School for welcoming me into their inner sanctum of coaching.

Thank you to the following folks for sharing their ideas about coaching: Jordan Bighorn, Anders Blomgren, Stephen Douglass, Tobin Fisher, Robin Haaseth, Brenda Holben, Albert Leal, Colleen Mahoney, Sharon Mast, Dori Monson, Kelly Pochop, Paris Pulford, Emily Roberts, Lisa Sheff, Guffrie Smith, Jr., Rudy Thomas, Paul Vidas, Missy Weirich, and Pamela Widmann.

Thank you to the following Web sites for providing me with information about coaching: Ken Chertow (www.kenchertow.com), Sports Physical Therapy Institute (www.sportspti.com), TeachersFirst (www.teachersfirst.com), and Y-Coach, Youth Coaching Information (www.y-coach.com).

Thank you to the following people who reviewed the manuscript: Tom Berkas, Chris Beyer, Bob Bierscheid, Brent Bolstrum, Stephanie Drakulich, Bill Kauffmann, Kathleen Kimball-Baker, Kathy McHugh, Augie Mendoza, Lisa Pitman, Emily Roberts, Guffrie M. Smith, Jr., Kathy Spangler, Joe Stewart, Ruth Taswell, and Nancy Tellett-Royce.

FOREWORD

Youth sports offer an endless series of teachable moments for the coach who is prepared to seize them. But all too often these opportunities are squandered by win-at-all-cost coaches who care only about the results on the scoreboard.

Using youth sports as a virtual classroom for life lessons requires what the Positive Coaching Alliance calls "Double-Goal Coaches™," who want to win *and* who have the even more important goal of using sports to teach life lessons and help kids develop positive character traits.

Grounded in Search Institute's research-based framework for youth development known as the 40 Developmental Assets, *Hey, Coach!* is an important resource for any coach who wants her or his players to win in all aspects of life.

Hey, Coach! is full of compelling case studies in which an initially daunting challenge is posed. Then the reader has the opportunity to reflect on how he or she would react in the same situation. A possible course of action is described and then analyzed with regard to the most salient of the 40 Developmental Assets.

The result is that *Hey, Coach!* provides a rich set of examples that can help inform decisions when faced with similar challenges in the course of a coaching career. These fictionalized case studies will help you act to ensure your players are having fun and learning new skills—not just in how to play the game but also in how to connect with others. And that will help them succeed in the larger game of life.

Hey, Coach! is an important tool for any coach and anyone who works with young people. Coaching is not a cookbook activity in which coaches follow a recipe precisely. Coaching kids is an art. *Hey, Coach!* provides some lovely hues for coaches who want to refine their artistry.

Jim Thompson
Founder, Positive Coaching Alliance
Author, *The Double-Goal Coach*

PREFACE

I grew up on Long Island listening to Mel Allen, Phil Rizzuto, and Red Barber broadcast Yankee games on WPIX Channel 11. As a preteen, I played in Little League—rather, I watched my teammates play from my vantage point on the bench. In school, I cursed President Kennedy for emphasizing that every student pass physical fitness tests. I remember bitterly envying my classmate, Roger Beinish, for somehow producing a lifelong doctor's excuse to get out of physical education class.

Through graduate school and beyond, I was an avid tennis player, but it wasn't until adulthood and participation on a volleyball team that I actually found pleasure from involvement in team sports. We called our volleyball team "No. 15 Plus Sausage" —a tribute to the pizza we invariably ordered at the Olympia Pizza and Spaghetti House after our games. More recently, I enjoyed the job of assistant coach for my son's coach-pitch team. My major duty consisted of maintaining a reasonable level of chaos in our dugout while everyone waited for a turn at bat.

I tell you this to illustrate that I'm not a sports nut by any means. (Though I do think that baseball is pretty much the perfect game, the character of many of its major league players notwithstanding.) However, I do recognize the value of sports and especially of coaches. My son, Cole, will be 9 years old when this book is published, and I would want him to experience all the caring from coaches that I espouse in this book. I want him to learn not only how to play baseball, soccer, and all the rest, but also how to treat his teammates and his opponents, how to suffer defeat and celebrate victory, how to balance his desires for winning and playing fair, and how to measure up to all the travails he'll face on and off the field. Much of this he can learn from his coaches, and much of it from coaches merely modeling how to behave.

I've developed many educational programs and written many books about education, prevention, and the like, but they always seem to come down to this: young people do better when adults care about them. The main character in this book—you, the reader—is given a whistle to help you reflect on various situations. On the whistle is printed "IT'S ABOUT THEM." The message refers to the young people with whom coaches come into contact every day. But the message could also be this: "IT'S ABOUT YOU." You are the ones who make it happen.

PREPARATION

You're the coach. But why? Why did you become a coach? Many of you might respond, "I like sports, I like teaching, and I like kids." But it's a lot deeper than that, isn't it? Think about all the issues sports touch on in some way: Discipline. Loyalty. Determination. Achievement. Fairness. Conflict. Aggression. Interpersonal dynamics. Drugs. Family. School. Personal futures. Young people play out these issues on basketball and volleyball courts, soccer and football fields, golf courses, baseball diamonds, wrestling mats, balance beams, tracks, and in swimming pools throughout their childhood and adolescence. As a coach, you're one of the stewards of these young people: you're in a position to help them address the issues in ways that allow young people to learn, mature, and thrive.

Yet coaches have difficult polarities seemingly built into their jobs: Win at all costs or make sure all players get equal playing time? Rule authoritatively or seek input from your players? Satisfy parents of the best players or satisfy all parents? Of course, it's rarely one or the other; nonetheless, coaches have to address these pressures.

If you're a good coach and a good teacher, you're most likely already doing things that help young people to build developmental assets—the positive skills, qualities, and experiences that young people need to succeed. You're to be congratulated—and motivated to persist. This book will give you a vocabulary to describe what you do and to assist you in doing it more intentionally.

Why did you become a coach? By the time you finish reading—finish participating in—this book, you may want to add some meaningful words to your original response.

Developmental Assets

This book is about addressing the issues you and your players face by helping them build Developmental Assets. These assets are the attitudes, behaviors, and experiences that help young people grow to be successful in both school and life. The researchers at Search Institute in Minneapolis, Minnesota, have identified 40 of these assets. Here we present the lists for students in grades 4 through 6 and adolescents. Most of the asset names are the same for both middle childhood and adolescence. The most significant difference between the two lists is the definitions; for example, they are more age appropriate.

Note that these 40 Developmental Assets divide evenly into 20 external and 20 internal assets. External assets identify important roles that families, schools, congregations, neighborhoods, and youth organizations can play in promoting healthy development; internal assets are those that reflect positive internal growth and development within young people. It should be emphasized, however, that people can't "import" either external or internal assets; they must build and nurture them themselves.

You'll also see that the assets are further arranged into eight categories: support, empowerment, boundaries and expectations, constructive use of time, commitment to learning, positive values, social competencies, and positive identity. This classification is intended to cluster the assets into areas of similarity. For example, creative activities and youth programs, assets 17 and 18, are both examples of constructive use of time while integrity and honesty, assets 28 and 29, are both positive values. Some assets are more important for some individuals—even some groups—than others. And some assets are realized in different ways, depending on the individuals and their circumstances. For me, caring, asset 26, might be realized by volunteering at a food bank once a month. For you, it might be realized in your day-to-day interactions with your colleagues. And for a young person, it might begin with taking a little extra time to ask a new student, "How are you doing?" (For one community's adaptation of the list of Developmental Assets specifically for coaches, see page 108, 40 Ways Coaches Can Build Assets for and with Youth.)

40 Developmental Assets for Middle Childhood
(Students in Grades 4 through 6)

EXTERNAL ASSETS

Support

1. **Family support**—Family life provides high levels of love and support.
2. **Positive family communication**—Parent(s) and child communicate positively. Child feels comfortable seeking advice and counsel from parent(s).
3. **Other adult relationships**—Child receives support from adults other than her or his parent(s).
4. **Caring neighborhood**—Child experiences caring neighbors.
5. **Caring school climate**—Relationships with teachers and peers provide a caring, encouraging school environment.
6. **Parent involvement in schooling**—Parent(s) are actively involved in helping the child succeed in school.

Empowerment

7. **Community values children**—Child feels valued and appreciated by the adults in the community.
8. **Children as resources**—Child is included in decisions at home and in the community.
9. **Service to others**—Child has opportunities to help others in the community.
10. **Safety**—Child feels safe at home, at school, and in her or his neighborhood.

Boundaries and Expectations

11. **Family boundaries**—Family has clear and consistent rules and consequences and monitors the child's whereabouts.
12. **School boundaries**—School provides clear rules and consequences.
13. **Neighborhood boundaries**—Neighbors take responsibility for monitoring the child's behavior.
14. **Adult role models**—Parent(s) and other adults in the child's family, as well as nonfamily adults, model positive, responsible behavior.
15. **Positive peer influence**—Child's closest friends model positive, responsible behavior.
16. **High expectations**—Parent(s) and teachers expect the child to do her or his best at school and in other activities.

Constructive Use of Time

17. **Creative activities**—Child participates in music, art, drama, or creative writing two or more times per week.
18. **Child programs**—Child participates two or more times per week in cocurricular activities or structured community programs for children.
19. **Religious community**—Child attends religious programs or services one or more times per week.
20. **Time at home**—Child spends some time most days both in high-quality interaction with parent(s) and doing things at home other than watching TV or playing video games.

(continues)

40 Developmental Assets for Middle Childhood
(Students in Grades 4 through 6)

INTERNAL ASSETS

Commitment to Learning

21. **Achievement motivation**—Child is motivated and strives to do well in school.
22. **Learning engagement**—Child is responsive, attentive, and actively engaged in learning at school and enjoys participating in learning activities outside of school.
23. **Homework**—Child usually hands in homework on time.
24. **Bonding to adults at school**—Child cares about teachers and other adults at school.
25. **Reading for pleasure**—Child enjoys and engages in reading for fun most days of the week.

Positive Values

26. **Caring**—Parent(s) tell the child it is important to help other people.
27. **Equality and social justice**—Parent(s) tell the child it is important to speak up for equal rights for all people.
28. **Integrity**—Parent(s) tell the child it is important to stand up for one's beliefs.
29. **Honesty**—Parent(s) tell the child it is important to tell the truth.
30. **Responsibility**—Parent(s) tell the child it is important to accept personal responsibility for behavior.
31. **Healthy lifestyle**—Parent(s) tell the child it is important to have good health habits and an understanding of healthy sexuality.

Social Competencies

32. **Planning and decision making**—Child thinks about decision making and is usually happy with the result of her or his decisions.
33. **Interpersonal competence**—Child cares about and is affected by other people's feelings, enjoys making friends, and, when frustrated or angry, tries to calm her- or himself.
34. **Cultural competence**—Child knows and is comfortable with people of different racial, ethnic, and cultural backgrounds and with her or his own cultural identity.
35. **Resistance skills**—Child can stay away from people who are likely to get her or him in trouble and is able to say no to doing wrong or dangerous things.
36. **Peaceful conflict resolution**—Child attempts to resolve conflict nonviolently.

Positive Identity

37. **Personal power**—Child feels he or she has some influence over things that happen in her or his life.
38. **Self-esteem**—Child likes and is proud to be the person he or she is.
39. **Sense of purpose**—Child sometimes thinks about what life means and whether there is a purpose for her or his life.
40. **Positive view of personal future**—Child is optimistic about her or his personal future.

40 Developmental Assets for Adolescents

EXTERNAL ASSETS

Support

1. **Family support**—Family life provides high levels of love and support.
2. **Positive family communication**—Young person and her or his parent(s) communicate positively, and young person is willing to seek advice and counsel from parent(s).
3. **Other adult relationships**—Young person receives support from three or more nonparent adults.
4. **Caring neighborhood**—Young person experiences caring neighbors.
5. **Caring school climate**—School provides a caring, encouraging environment.
6. **Parent involvement in schooling**—Parent(s) are actively involved in helping young person succeed in school

Empowerment

7. **Community values youth**—Young person perceives that adults in the community value youth.
8. **Youth as resources**—Young people are given useful roles in the community.
9. **Service to others**—Young person serves in the community one hour or more per week.
10. **Safety**—Young person feels safe at home, at school, and in the neighborhood.

Boundaries and Expectations

11. **Family boundaries**—Family has clear rules and consequences, and monitors the young person's whereabouts.
12. **School boundaries**—School provides clear rules and consequences.
13. **Neighborhood boundaries**—Neighbors take responsibility for monitoring young people's behavior.
14. **Adult role models**—Parent(s) and other adults model positive, responsible behavior.
15. **Positive peer influence**—Young person's best friends model responsible behavior.
16. **High expectations**—Both parent(s) and teachers encourage the young person to do well.

Constructive Use of Time

17. **Creative activities**—Young person spends three or more hours per week in lessons or practice in music, theater, or other arts.
18. **Youth programs**—Young person spends three or more hours per week in sports, clubs, or organizations at school and/or in the community.
19. **Religious community**—Young person spends one or more hours per week in activities in a religious institution.
20. **Time at home**—Young person is out with friends "with nothing special to do" two or fewer nights per week.

(continues)

40 Developmental Assets for Adolescents

INTERNAL ASSETS

Commitment to Learning

21. **Achievement motivation**—Young person is motivated to do well in school.
22. **School engagement**—Young person is actively engaged in learning.
23. **Homework**—Young person reports doing at least one hour of homework every school day.
24. **Bonding to school**—Young person cares about her or his school.
25. **Reading for pleasure**—Young person reads for pleasure three or more hours per week.

Positive Values

26. **Caring**—Young person places high value on helping other people.
27. **Equality and social justice**—Young person places high value on promoting equality and reducing hunger and poverty.
28. **Integrity**—Young person acts on convictions and stands up for her or his beliefs.
29. **Honesty**—Young person "tells the truth even when it is not easy."
30. **Responsibility**—Young person accepts and takes personal responsibility.
31. **Restraint**—Young person believes it is important not to be sexually active or to use alcohol or other drugs.

Social Competencies

32. **Planning and decision making**—Young person knows how to plan ahead and make choices.
33. **Interpersonal competence**—Young person has empathy, sensitivity, and friendship skills.
34. **Cultural competence**—Young person has knowledge of and comfort with people of different cultural/racial/ethnic backgrounds.
35. **Resistance skills**—Young person can resist negative peer pressure and dangerous situations.
36. **Peaceful conflict resolution**—Young person seeks to resolve conflict nonviolently.

Positive Identity

37. **Personal power**—Young person feels he or she has control over "things that happen to me."
38. **Self-esteem**—Young person reports having a high self-esteem.
39. **Sense of purpose**—Young person reports that "my life has a purpose."
40. **Positive view of personal future**—Young person is optimistic about her or his personal future.

The Importance of Developmental Assets

Why are Developmental Assets important? They've been shown in surveys of more than one million young people as being positively associated with young people's success in school—academic success, social success, and the avoidance of high-risk behaviors such as drug use, violence, and early sexual activity. In short, the more assets young people report having, the more likely they're growing up healthy. The following charts show the relationships between assets and behaviors quite clearly.

Building Developmental Assets

How do we help young people build these assets? We do it intentionally in three major ways: by forming and maintaining strong, genuine, supportive relationships with young people; by providing an environment in which they feel that they matter; and by facilitating programs and practices that give them opportunities to thrive. (For some quick tips on building Developmental Assets with your players, see page 116, Asset-Building Ideas for Coaches.)

This is where you come in. Coaches are in the tremendously important position to foster those relationships, to provide that environment, and to facilitate those programs and practices. When students form relationships with school adults—such as coaches—as well as with peers, then they're not only helping build asset 24, bonding to school, but they're also laying a strong foundation for building many of the other assets, such as asset 33, interpersonal competence, and asset 37, personal power. You as a coach can make a positive difference and have a strong impact on how the young people you work with grow up and mature. You are the ones they'll remember as special when they're adults.

The Power of Assets to Protect from High-Risk Behaviors

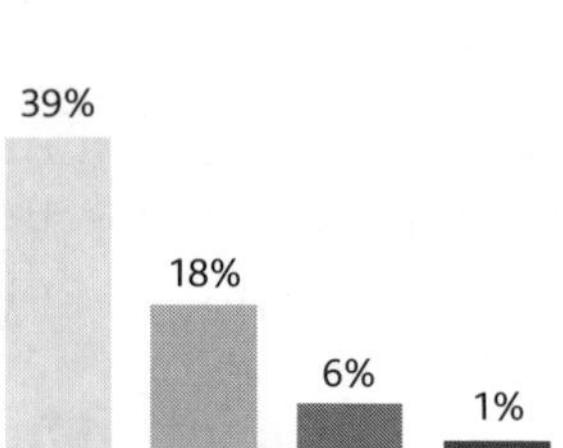

Illicit Drug Use

Used illicit drugs (marijuana, cocaine, LSD, PCP/angel dust, heroin, or amphetamines) three or more times in the past 12 months.

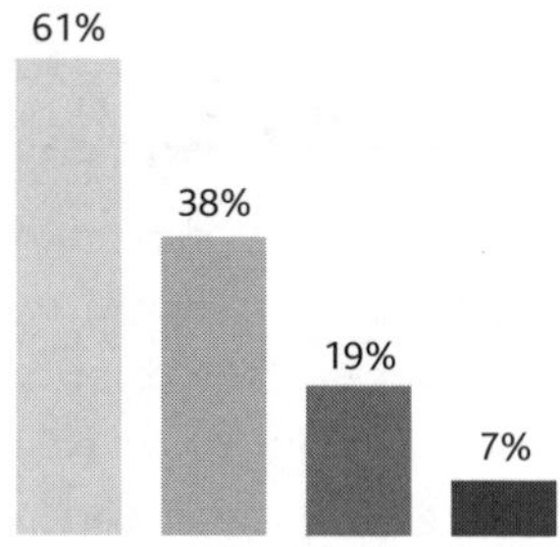

Violence

Has engaged in three or more acts of fighting, hitting, injuring a person, carrying a weapon, or threatening physical harm in the past 12 months.

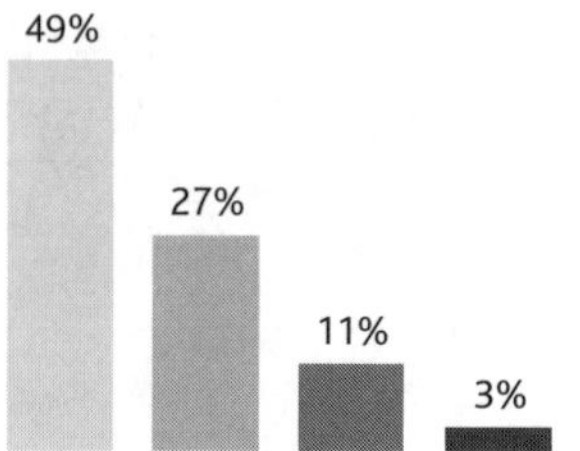

Problem Alcohol Use

Has used alcohol three or more times in the past 30 days or got drunk once or more in the past two weeks.

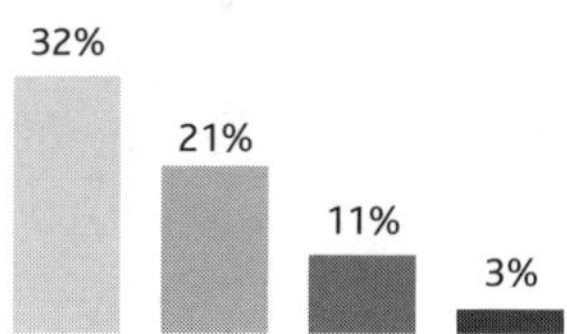

Sexual Activity

Has had sexual intercourse three or more times in lifetime.

These data are based on surveys during the 1999–2000 school year of 217,277 students in 6th through 12th grade public and private U.S. schools.

The Power of Assets to Promote Positive Attitudes and Behaviors

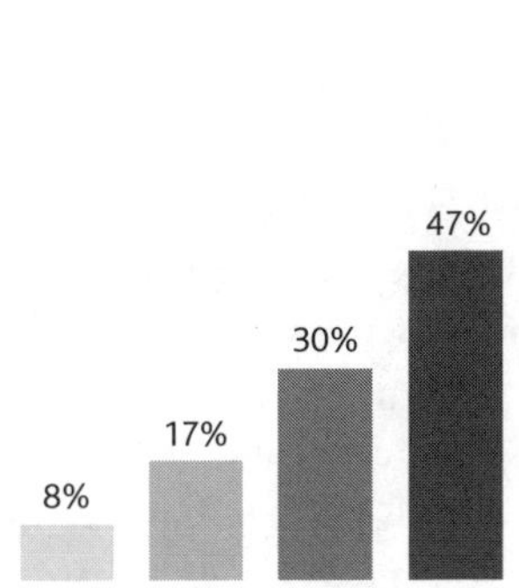

Succeeds in School

Gets mostly A's on report card (an admittedly high standard).

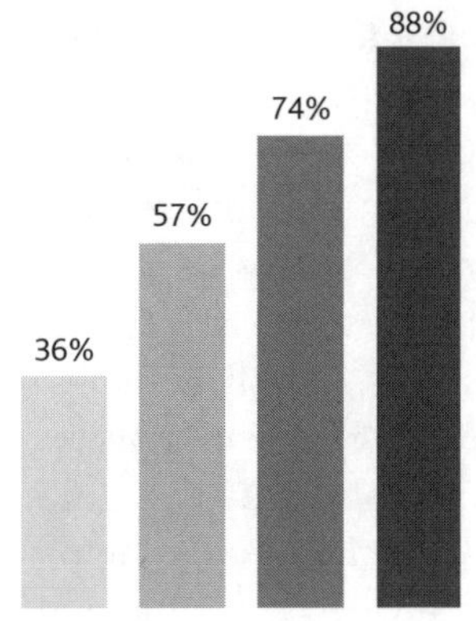

Values Diversity

Thinks it is important to get to know people of other racial/ethnic groups.

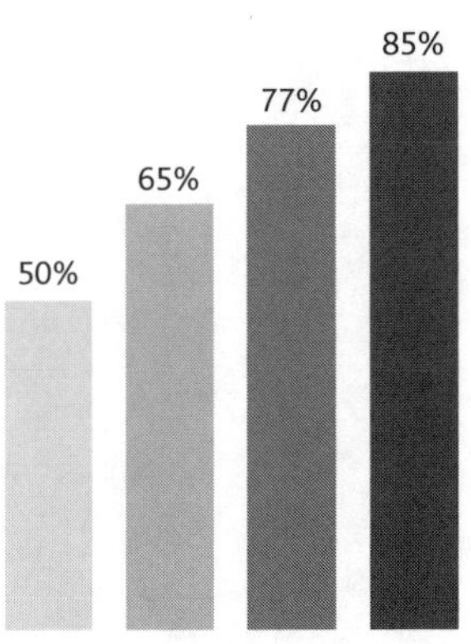

Exhibits Leadership

Has been a leader of an organization or group in the past 12 months.

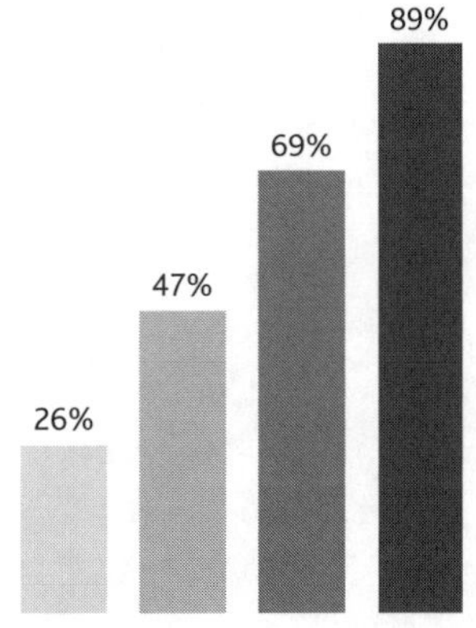

Maintains Good Health

Takes good care of body (such as eating foods that are healthy and exercising regularly).

These data are based on surveys during the 1999–2000 school year of 217,277 students in 6th through 12th grade public and private U.S. schools.

What You'll Find in This Book

In these pages you'll find 19 fictionalized situations to test you as a coach. What would you do in each circumstance? Before each situation, I'll tell you which asset—or assets—to try to promote. When you read these situations, try to put yourself into the action. Think about what you would do, what you would say, and how you would say it—before you continue reading. How would you promote assets to make a positive impact on the young people entrusted to you?

Consider this book as a kind of virtual-reality training. While at least one response is provided for every situation, your own response(s) may be just as good or better. All the situations are fictitious, so there's no "true" solution. After each group of three situations, you'll actually have the opportunity to debrief in a "huddle" that will give you a chance to mull over a variety of issues presented by the situations.

You'll have some help along the way. I'm giving you a whistle. On the whistle are the words "IT'S ABOUT THEM." That's it: "IT'S ABOUT THEM." Remember that, and you'll do fine.

WARM-UP

THE CHAOTIC CLASS

* * *

Physical education class

Sacajawea Elementary School

Burlington, Tennessee

Asset 12—School boundaries

Dividing the class into hula-hoopers, scarf-jugglers, ball-tossers, and free-dancers seemed like a good idea, but things are now a bit out of hand. You actually encourage a certain amount of yelling and horseplay—it provides positive energy in the gym. But the yelling has given way to screaming and the horseplay to scuffling.

You consider whistling to quiet down the group, but just then you notice that the ball Allen Hastings was tossing has found its way to the very middle of the scarf-jugglers—and they're not stopping for him to retrieve it. Allen is not noted for his patience. You rush over in time to see him knock over one of the jugglers.

"Hey! Wait until I'm finished, why don't you!" the juggler yells.

"I waited! You wouldn't let me in!"

"You just had to wait until I was finished! I was going for a record!"

"So what? I can't wait forever!"

Out of the corner of your eye, you spy a red hula hoop rolling toward the dancers and Bron Livingston yelling "Incoming!" and bursting into laughter. One of the dancers rolls her eyes in disgust and hurls the hula hoop back to Bron. Meanwhile, Patricia Sard, whose personality is as fragile as a flower, is huddled by the bleachers, her face buried in her arms.

Before you can check in on either of these situations you hear Andrew Osaki complaining as usual. "Would you stop throwing it so hard!"

He explains to you with an indignation usually reserved for adults, "He's either throwing it so I can't get it or throwing it right at my face!"

"I am not!" retorts Jeff Park, his partner. "He just can't catch!"

"I can if you throw it to me!"

"I was!"

"You were not!"

"I was so!"

You think again of blowing your whistle, just to get everyone settled down, but then the bell rings. Most of the students stop as if punctured, and you remind them to return the equipment to its proper place. For the most part, they do and scamper out. Only a few escape without tending to their hula hoops and balls.

As you pick up the items not put away, you make a note to find out what's going on with Patricia Sard.

So what should the plan be next time? A little horseplay turned into chaos, and order needed to be restored. What's the best plan for tomorrow?

YOU'RE THE COACH!

WHAT WOULD YOU DO?

Think about the situation as if you were there yourself, particularly in terms of the **school boundaries** asset. **How would you establish guidelines while still respecting your students?** How would you handle the situation to promote assets and make a positive impact?

This isn't hard at all, you think. The class needs a plan or a code—a list of rules as well as the consequences for breaking them.

So you go about creating those rules. You jot down some notes while thinking about what you want to accomplish in the class. You work with those notes in the evening and come up with five simple rules:

1. **Be polite.** At appropriate times, say "please," "thank you," and "excuse me."
2. **Include others.** If you see that someone is not participating, invite that person to join in. Share equipment so that everyone gets a turn.
3. **Use language to solve problems.** Don't yell. Speak in a conversational tone, and try to work out conflicts peacefully.
4. **Ask an adult for help.** If you can't solve a problem yourself, ask an adult to assist you.
5. **Stay safe.** Never do anything that would endanger yourself or someone else.

Consequences for breaking these rules: first offense in a day—sit out 5 minutes; second offense—sit out 10 minutes; third offense—sit out entire period. All time-outs will be carried over to the following day until they've been completed.

The next morning, you arrive at school early and make a poster of the rules, using alternating colors so that each rule stands out. This is asset 12, you think to yourself: school boundaries. You're providing clear rules and consequences, and you're promoting asset 12. You really are a good P.E. teacher.

You've experienced the warm-up situation. Now let me try to anticipate some of your questions:

So how did I do?

How do you think you did?

Pretty good, I think. Chaos reigned in the class. No one knew the rules. No one was necessarily bad; the students just didn't have any boundaries.

And so . . .

And so I remembered asset 12, school boundaries, and made some for them.

Why did you do that?

Because they needed rules and consequences.

How do you know that the rules and consequences were appropriate?

Well, hmm . . . I guess because I'm an adult. I'm a teacher and a coach. I have more experience than the kids do, which means I know what's best for them. Wait a minute, I messed up. The rules and consequences were a good idea, but I wasn't using a process consistent with building assets.

What could you have done differently?

I could have presented the students with the situation and gotten them to acknowledge that we were having some problems. I could have said, "Remember what happened yesterday? Allen got into an argument, and Bron interfered with some of the dancers. Patricia was sitting by herself, and Andrew and Jeff were having some differences about who was throwing what to whom—remember all that?"

And then?

Then I could have asked the students what they thought should happen, and we could have developed the rules and consequences together. Or at least I could have written up the rules and consequences and asked them their thoughts on changes or additions.

That would have taken quite a bit of time.

Yes, it would have—time that I really didn't have. But in the long run, it probably would have been worth it because the students would presumably be more likely to pay attention to rules that they had a hand in making. The main point is that they would have felt not just part of the problem but also part of the solution.

Anything else?

I might have messed up. But at least I figured out how *I messed up.*

This warm-up illustrates that what sometimes appears to be the best solution is often only the most efficient solution—the two are not always the same. The idea is to find the best solution for your students—in the long run, the best solution for you as well.

Now you'll encounter 18 situations that you might face as a coach. I've divided them into six "periods":

- First Period—Teammates;
- Second Period—Families;
- Third Period—Communities;
- Fourth Period—Society;
- Fifth Period—Attitudes; and
- Sixth Period—Performance.

After each period, we'll have a "huddle" to discuss your responses and the issues in general. After the last situation, we'll meet in the "locker room" to review the whole experience.

The first three situations will concern teammates—students who, for one reason or another, don't get along with their fellow players. Are you ready?

Let's play ball!

FIRST 1 PERIOD

TEAMMATES

SITUATION 1: THE DISGRUNTLED QUARTERBACK

* * *

Football practice

Tumwater High School

Portland, Oregon

Asset 8—Youth as resources

Asset 22—School engagement

"Three!"

Jack spins, grunts, and heaves the ball 30 yards downfield into the gray sky, where seconds later Peter lets the spiral bounce off his midsection with another grunt. The ball wobbles away, and Peter shakes his head as he fetches it.

"Almost, Peter!" you yell. And to Jack, who's closer to you: "Nice throw, Jack, except Peter's number two; *Achmed's* number three."

Jack takes Peter's toss and slams the ball into the ground. "Two, three—this is stupid! This is a stupid drill! And no one can catch the ball, anyway! What's the difference?"

The drill is called "set, find, and fire." You set up four receivers downfield—"one," "two," "three," and "four"—and at regular intervals you call out one of the numbers. The idea is for your quarterback to quickly identify the appropriate receiver, set up, and accurately throw the football. Jack is a good quarterback—at least in terms of his ability—but his relationship with his teammates is poor.

"Don't blame me if you can't tell your numbers apart," says Peter, who naturally has taken offense at Jack's comment.

Jack responds with an anatomical command, and you decide to call it a day.

"Something wrong?" you ask Jack later. This has become your routine after Monday practice. You ask Jack how he's doing. He responds with a complaint against someone or something. You ask him how you can help, and he says that he'll be all right by Friday.

Jack Salton is actually a good kid. And he really does care about his teammates. You know this because you've seen him do generous things for them, even anonymously. For example, he once gave you several Internet links about weight control and asked you to pass them on to Joseph, your center, who was having problems keeping his weight down. And another time he made sure that everyone signed a birthday card to give to Randy, the fullback.

In a way, though, even those acts were self-centered: Jack depends on a strong center and a happy fullback to do his own job well. It's tough being a quarterback—everything is really about you. All his life, Jack has been the center of attention. He's an only child, he's extremely athletic, he's popular, and he does well in school. But he's also a prima donna who's impatient with his teammates, especially those who have fewer abilities than he does. You've talked with Mr. Salton, and he has high expectations for his son.

"There's nothing wrong," Jack says now as he changes back into street clothes. "I'm just a little tired, and I'm also tired of people not giving it their all."

"Anyone in particular?"

"You know who I'm talking about. I bust my butt out there. I follow the rules, I do my stuff, and I expect everyone else to do the same. That's what's going to make us a good team."

"Jack, can you tell the difference between someone trying really hard but not doing everything perfectly and someone else not trying very hard at all but doing pretty well?"

"What?"

"I think that everyone's giving it as much as they can, but not everyone has the same ability."

"Yeah, whatever. See you later, Coach."

YOU'RE THE COACH!

WHAT WOULD YOU DO?

Think about the situation as if you were there yourself, particularly in terms of the **youth as resources** and **school engagement** assets. **How would you address Jack's concerns as well as his relationships with his teammates?** How would you handle the situation in a way that would promote assets and make a positive impact?

You think Jack needs to be in a situation where he's giving something to someone or doing something for someone, and not only because in the end it would benefit him. It would also be good for Jack to be in a situation where he had to work with someone who wasn't as capable as he was. He needs to see that some people try really hard but can't always achieve the way he can. If he were placed in those situations, then maybe he'd have a healthier attitude toward his teammates, maybe even a healthier attitude toward people in general.

What are situations like those, you wonder.

You call the school counselor, Ms. Hobbes, and tell her your idea. She thinks it's great.

"But would Jack go for it?" she asks. He's probably got his plate full already."

"I'll ask him. I think he'd have time for this. Whether he'd want to do it is another question."

It's not until after Wednesday practice that you're able to sit down with Jack in the athletic office. Each of you takes a chair, and you tell him your idea. He reacts with some confusion.

"You want me to be a tutor?"

"Only if *you* want to. I think it's a good idea."

"What would I have to do?"

"You can work out the details with Ms. Hobbes, but essentially you'd be helping kids in one of the elementary schools with their reading and writing. I don't have any more details than that, but tell me this: Are you interested?"

"Wouldn't it take away from practice time?"

"A little. But I think the experience would be worth it."

Jack slumps in his chair. You think that maybe he's insulted.

"This is some sort of punishment, isn't it?"

"Not at all. Why do you say that?"

"Because I've been mouthing off about some of the guys, and you want to show me my place."

You'd forgotten how reflective Jack could be.

"Actually, Jack, I've been thinking about how much you really have to give, and that's why I recommended you to Ms. Hobbes. You know a lot, but you don't often have the opportunity to share your knowledge with others. This will give you that opportunity. It will also help some younger kids who will look up to you. I'm hoping that the experience will also teach you to have more patience with people who don't share your strengths. Honestly, I think doing this will help you feel better about yourself and better about your teammates."

"You think I don't feel good about myself?"

"I think you waver."

Jack smiles. "Would anyone on the team know I was doing this?"

"That's up to you."

He gets up, shakes your hand, and heads for the door.

"Yeah, I guess you can tell Ms. Hobbes I might consider it. I wouldn't want to deprive some second-grader of the chance to get tutored by the great Jack Salton."

The door closes. You retreat to your desk and begin working on tomorrow's practice schedule.

SITUATION 2: THE QUIET TEAMMATE

* * *

Volleyball practice

Mark Twain Junior High School

Selkirk, Missouri

Asset 17—Creative activities

Asset 33—Interpersonal competence

You're trying really hard not to take sides, but you can see why the team is having problems with Melinda.

She's a very competent setter. Right now you're standing on the other side of the net from Melinda and a few of her teammates. You're working on an exercise to help the setter read the defense of the opposing team. Someone in the back row tosses the ball to Melinda. You hold up either rock, paper, or scissors, and Melinda has to yell out what you're holding before setting the ball to a hitter in the front row. She's performing just fine, but she shows no excitement, no enthusiasm. She barely yells "rock," and after the set she displays no emotion.

Her lack of emotion is driving the others crazy.

Katie is beside herself. She says under her breath, "It's like she graces us with her presence because she has nothing else more important to do. Why does she even come here? Do her parents *make* her play?"

The truth is, Melinda might just be the most accomplished player on the team, but she's quiet. And reserved. Melinda's other interests include creative writing, math, and weaving. She doesn't laugh much, and she seems embarrassed by compliments. She performs her duties well but quietly. Melinda is apparently one of those introspective people who do just fine in the world but who sometimes put others on edge.

You've tried talking with Melinda. You've asked her about her interests outside volleyball. You've joked with her. You've complimented her. You've even given her some extra responsibilities to see if that would help her interact more with the others. But each of your efforts has met with only limited success.

"What do you want me to do?" you ask Katie one afternoon after she's complained yet again about Melinda's seeming indifference. "She's not unfriendly, she's not selfish, she's not sloppy. She's a great player. She just has a different sense of things."

"She has *no* sense of things! If she did, she'd get excited, pound her fist after a good play, hold her head after she messed up. Curse! Something!"

"Would you like me to set up a meeting, so you can tell her how you feel?"

Katie pauses. "I don't want to cause any trouble."

"It's not any trouble. It's for the team."

"Okay. But what are you going to say?" Katie asks.

"I'll call a team meeting and ask if anyone has any problems they'd like to talk about. Then you can say what you want—as long as it's not deliberately hurtful, of course—and maybe others will, too."

Katie thinks about this. "Okay. That might be good. Maybe I'm missing something. Maybe it's me."

The following week, halfway through practice, you sit the girls down by the bleachers and ask if anyone has anything they'd like to talk about. No one says a word. You glance at Katie, who sighs.

"Well," she says, "sometimes I think that a few of us aren't always giving it our all, you know, like getting excited about stuff."

You wait for a response—from anyone—but there is none.

Finally, you ask, "Does anyone agree with that?"

Carmen raises her hand. "Yeah, I think that sometimes."

That's it. No one talks. Melinda is gazing at her shoes.

"Melinda?" you say. "Susie? Evie? Anyone have any thoughts about that? Is there anyone who feels that she might try harder than she is?"

Again, nothing.

"Okay," you say. "Maybe it's hard for people to talk in this setting. Why don't we get back to practice. But if anyone has anything to say to me in private, they can do that."

After practice two interesting things happen. One is that you become acutely aware of what's written on your whistle: "IT'S ABOUT THEM." Yes, you think, that's true: this is about them, the team, the individuals. You knew that.

The second interesting thing is that Melinda comes to your office and asks to speak to you. You motion for her to sit down, and you move your chair out from behind your desk. You ask Melinda what's on her mind.

"I'm not stupid," she begins, slowly, not making eye contact. "I know they think that I don't try."

"Your teammates?"

She nods.

"And?"

"They're right. Sort of."

"What do you mean?"

Melinda looks at you for the first time. "I don't yell and scream and get pumped up like they do. But I do the best I can. That's just the way I am. Athletic stuff—comes easy to me. And . . . I don't know."

You wait, but Melinda appears to be finished. "Do you enjoy playing volleyball, Melinda?"

She looks at you again, this time much more directly. "Yes, I like it a lot. I like all sports. I like playing, and I like winning, and I kind of like being on a team. But just because I don't act like everyone else doesn't mean I'm some kind of, I don't know, loser."

Another pause. "Why don't you tell that to your teammates, Melinda? They're good kids; I think they'd understand. They're just misinterpreting you. I could tell them, but I don't think it would mean as much."

Melinda shakes her head. "I could never do that."

YOU'RE THE COACH!

WHAT WOULD YOU DO?

Think about the situation as if you were there yourself, particularly in terms of the **creative activities** and **interpersonal competence** assets. **How would you help Melinda become more a part of the team while respecting her individuality?** How would you handle the situation in a way that would promote assets and make a positive impact?

"Melinda," you say, "you like to write, don't you."

Melinda nods.

"Why don't you use your writing to explain to your teammates how you feel?"

She frowns.

"Maybe you create a story, maybe a play, maybe a poem. The main thing is for Katie and the others to appreciate not only what you do, but also how you do it. I *know* that you can get them to understand this way."

"But that sounds so . . . dorky."

"It's up to you, of course. But I think you'll find that your teammates *want* to understand you. I don't think they'll find you dorky. Why don't you at least think about it."

Melinda nods and abruptly leaves. You determine not to let the issue founder but to follow up with it in a week or so.

By that time, however, the problem seems to have been resolved. You notice more smiles on the court, even occasionally from Melinda. The girls actually joke with her. The total result is more energy.

After a workout, you corral Katie. "What happened?" you ask.

Katie swigs some water. "Melinda wrote this really cool story. Well, the first part of a story. She's going to add more to it every week. It was sort of about her, and it's really good. I guess it kind of explained what she's about. It made me realize that she's more okay than I thought she was. You know."

You nod. "Can I see the story?"

Katie smiles, lowers the water bottle, and heads to the locker room. "Sorry," she calls back. "Only for the team."

You'd really like to see what Melinda wrote, you think, as everyone heads out of the gym. But then you remember what it says on your whistle, and you shrug it off and head for the lockers.

SITUATION 3: THE SPORT OF FIGHTING?

* * *

No Holds Barred Wrestling Club

Sam Hill Basin, Iowa

Asset 35—Resistance skills

Asset 36—Peaceful conflict resolution

Adam and Griffin don't like each other much, period. You've seen a collision coming for a month now, but you've felt like a helpless bystander watching two trains heading right toward each other.

Maybe the tension has something to do with socioeconomic status. Maybe it has something to do with personality styles. Or, maybe there's just something in people—a sort of built-in alarm system—that reacts adversely to certain other people.

Adam Watson is well-mannered, well-to-do, and well-educated, and he lets everyone know it. Griffin Soriano is tough. He's had to struggle for everything he's received, and *he* lets everyone know it, too. From the first day of the six-week course, you've sensed the impending clash. First came little comments, some less direct than others. (Adam: "I don't know how anyone could fail to understand the mechanics of the knee-spin sweep attack." Griffin: "You'd have to be pretty desperate to try a headlock in *that* position.") Then came the slights—Adam not acknowledging Griffin after a drill match, Griffin inviting two boys to sit with him for a snack and pointedly not asking Adam.

You tell yourself that's fine—not everyone has to like everyone else. But the tension has increased, and the whole class is aware of it.

Today the trains collide.

It happens during "monkey fighting." All the wrestlers hunch down in a squat, trying to push and shove their opponents to their knees or their rear. The exercise is a great workout for the legs, for balance, and for agility. You have 12 wrestlers, and you usually have them go at each other in a free-for-all. The last one squatting is the winner.

Today, Griffin goes straight past two potential opponents and pushes Adam to the mat from behind. It's all perfectly legitimate, if a bit underhanded.

Adam is furious.

"You coward!" he screams when he realizes who has shoved him down. "Do that to my face!"

"No problem!" says Griffin, lunging for him. The boys are immediately entangled. You automatically go for your whistle, but think better of it. The other boys are surrounding and cheering one or the other of the combatants, who are now not only wrestling but also hitting and kicking. You dive in and with a lot of effort and a little help from your assistant and one or two of the boys, you manage to separate Adam and Griffin.

"Let 'em fight!" you hear as you take each of them by the arm and lead them back to your office. Your assistant restores order and gets the rest of the boys back to the drill.

YOU'RE THE COACH!

WHAT WOULD YOU DO?

Think about the situation as if you were there yourself, particularly in terms of the **resistance skills** and **peaceful conflict resolution** assets. **How would you resolve the conflict between Griffin and Adam? Is it unreasonable to think that boys engaged in a sport would settle their differences in any other way?** How would you handle the situation in a way that would promote assets and make a positive impact?

You sit Adam and Griffin down on the bench in your office. You sit across from them on a chair.

"Well?" you say.

"He's a punk!" spits out Adam. "Only a punk would go for a cheap shot like that!"

"I didn't do anything you haven't done before," says Griffin, a little more sullen yet more in control. "You think a wrestler's always going to stand in front of you and let you take him down?" He snorts disgustedly.

"Okay, okay," you say. "I think we all know that this goes beyond the little scrap you boys just participated in. You've been after each other from the start. What's the problem?"

Neither boy talks.

You sigh. "I know you've heard this a thousand times before, but fighting is not going to solve whatever your problem is."

Griffin looks up sharply. "Hey, why do you think I'm in this club? Why are you even coaching this class? It's to make us better fighters, isn't it?" You notice Adam rolling his eyes.

"No, it's not," you say. "This class is meant to help you become more competent in the sport of wrestling."

"Same thing!" says Griffin. "It's to make us more competent fighters. What are you talking about? This ain't no sport. This ain't football or b-ball. We're fighting, man! Maybe prissy little prep boys"—he looks deliberately at Adam—"like to tell themselves it's a sport, but you ask all the guys out there"—he gestures back to the gym—"if they cared whether we went by the rules or not or whether they just wanted to see me pound pretty-boy's butt into the ground. Wrestling is fighting, man."

Again, think about the situation. Have your actions changed anything for Griffin and Adam? What would you do?

Your whistle says "IT'S ABOUT THEM." But this situation is becoming about you. You wonder if you're deluding yourself. By training young men in wrestling, are you really introducing them to an age-old sport, getting them into better physical condition, and teaching them some fun and creative ways of participating in athletics? Or are you really just giving them new weapons with which to hurt each other?

"I want to talk to each of you about what this underlying problem might be," you say. "But first I want to talk to you about wrestling. Griffin, do you really believe that being a better fighter will make you safer?"

Griffin replies as if he's talking to a second-grader. "Duh, yeah."

"'Duh' is right," says Adam.

"Listen," you say, "have you ever seen an instance in which fighting solved a problem?"

"Happens all the time."

"Can you give me an example?"

Griffin grins. "When was the last time you saw a hockey game? And even in football and b-ball—you think the refs catch every penalty?"

You shake your head. He's missed the point. "Griffin, I'm not saying fighting doesn't happen. What I'm saying is that it's not effective. And to the extent it is effective, I don't believe it's worth it. Look, let's suppose you do get in a fight and you do use your superior wrestling skills to your advantage. What if that person returns the next day with a couple of his friends? What if that person approaches you later with a knife or a gun? And Adam, I'm talking to you, too."

"Hey, I didn't do anything! A guy can defend himself, can't he?"

"I'm talking about the future. Do you honestly think that Olympic wrestlers are tough guys who constantly get into fights? Wrestling *is* a sport, not a way to solve problems.

"Here's what I want both of you to do. I want you to think of an example—any example—in which fighting solved a problem. Come back to me with it, if you can think of something, and we'll talk about it. And I want you to do something else, too—something a lot more difficult. I want you to stand up to the pressure to fight. Even if your friends say you should, I want you to resist. Being strong means *not* fighting, get it?"

Both Adam and Griffin are silent now. You don't know whether you're getting to them or they're just bored.

"Next time you're here, I'm going to give you some skills for resolving your conflicts peacefully," you say. "Real conflict resolution has to do with asking the other person, essentially, 'What's your problem?', and then trying to work it out through discussion. Can I get your commitment to at least try this?"

"Sure," they both say quietly.

"You're my best wrestlers," you say. "How about returning to the sport?"

They nod and leave your office. You feel that you have a long way to go with them, but at least you've started on the path.

(For a handout to help you resolve conflict among your teammembers, see *Pass It On at School! Activity Handouts for Creating Caring Schools* by Jeanne Engelmann, Activity Handout #65—Anger Rising, Conflict Solutions 101.)

HUDDLE

INSTANT REPLAY

THE PROBLEM	THE ASSET-BUILDING SOLUTION
A player doesn't think that other teammates are playing their best.	• Help build asset 8, youth as resources, and asset 22, school engagement. • Set up a mentoring situation for the player so that he can see how people with limited abilities really do try.
A quiet player isn't connecting with her teammates.	• Help build asset 17, creative activities, and asset 33, interpersonal competence. • Encourage the quiet player to use her interest in writing to create a story about herself to share with teammates.
Two teammates can't get along and eventually engage in a fistfight.	• Help build asset 35, resistance skills, and asset 36, peaceful conflict resolution. • Talk directly with your players and get them to commit to resolve conflicts peacefully.

Asset Referee: Let's discuss the three situations that you've just experienced. Did you have any problems?

Asset-Building Coach: *These situations are so short-lived; I don't stay around long enough in one place to find out if I'm doing okay in terms of promoting assets.*

AR: The real world can be like that, too. It may take quite a while before we know if we've been effective. Sometimes we never know. Building assets is like planting seeds that we hope will germinate and blossom.

ABC: *Let me tell you some other things that have been bothering me. I'm not sure that setting up Jack to be a mentor was the best thing I could have done. I mean, maybe he wasn't the right person for mentoring. Maybe he wasn't caring enough. Maybe he wasn't even smart enough.*

AR: Of course, that's possible. No doubt you could have made some other suggestions to help him realize his potential. But every option means taking a chance. Jack may just as easily have become a great mentor, helping children *and* himself. He probably wouldn't have thought of mentoring by himself. You were able to expand his ideas about himself and what he could do.

ABC: *I'm also wondering about Melinda. I did get her to use her creative abilities to communicate her feelings to her teammates, and that seemed to work out. But in some ways that felt a little indirect. Maybe I should have just sat her down with her teammates and tried a little harder to get her to talk.*

AR: That strategy may have gotten her to open up, but there's a chance it could have pushed her further away—perhaps even off the team. Given her strengths and the needs of the situation, you chose well. You helped promote her assets as well as those of her teammates: they'll be better able to form friendships with each other.

ABC: *It would be nice to know for sure.*

AR: Yes, it would. What about the other situation—the boys who were fighting?

ABC: *The situation with Adam and Griffin is troubling.*

AR: Why?

ABC: *I know there's a difference between wrestling and fighting to beat someone up. But in wrestling, and in boxing, the violence is the point. It's not incidental, like in football or basketball.*

AR: I'm not sure that violence is the *point,* but it's certainly the only means to the end of defeating one's opponent. Thinking is also a factor, but you can't win a wrestling match merely by out-thinking your opponent; somewhere along the line, you have to fight.

ABC: *And so . . .*

AR: And so that's why many people don't think that wrestling and especially boxing are appropriate activities—for young people or for adults.

ABC: *So it's an open question.*

AR: It is for some people.

ABC: *Another aspect of that situation that's bothering me is what to do with the two boys who were fighting. I talked with them, but I'm not sure that I convinced them that fighting doesn't solve problems. They have so many examples where fighting is used to solve problems—bullies who get money from younger students, men who overpower women, nations who defeat weaker countries . . .*

AR: You're saying that the world is imperfect, and you'd like it to be better. That's why we're promoting assets. Remember that you're not building assets *for* young people; you're helping them build assets for themselves. But for a variety of reasons, sometimes your efforts don't reap the rewards you'd like.

Young people have a variety of models to choose from. Some, unfortunately, are going to choose ones that will get them in trouble; others are going to choose ones that will help them be moral, productive, happy citizens. You can't guarantee anything. What you *can* do is give young people the information and skills to help them. Consider the alternative.

ABC: *I'm ready for the next set of situations.*

AR: The next three situations concern families. You'll be responding to a parent angry about a decision in a ball game, some parents who don't know each other very well, and a parent who's concerned about her daughter's grades. Are you ready?

ABC: *I'm ready.*

SECOND 2 PERIOD

FAMILIES

SITUATION 4: THE ANGRY PARENT

* * *

Basketball game

Birch Bayh High School

Fostick, Indiana

Asset 14—Adult role models

Even as you're giving the last-minute—last-second—instructions, you can't help but think that this is the fun part of coaching—using your players to the best advantage in order to squeak out a win. One more basket and the game is yours. One more win and the league championship is yours. Your starters are huddled around you in this last time-out, but you're screaming to be heard over the din of the home crowd. Everyone is shouting, "Hor-*nets*! Hor-*nets*! Hor-*nets*!" The scoreboard gives evidence to the direness of the situation: a score of 55-54, in favor of the rival Carson High Wolverines. You squat before the earnest faces of the five boys who will carry out your orders.

Simpson is the logical choice to get the in-bounds pass because he's the best ball-handler. And Daly is the logical choice to try to get open and take the shot because he's your purest shooter. But the Wolverines know this and so most likely will be double-teaming Daly, who doesn't shoot well under pressure. Your big man, Shelton, might be able to take a position under the basket, but it's uncertain whether either Simpson or Daly would be able to get the ball to him. You'd prefer not giving either Sweet or Markovich the ball in this situation. And you have only four seconds—not enough time for more than one or two passes at most.

You give them the percentage play: "Pass the ball in to Simpson, who will get it to Daly. If Daly isn't open, then pass it to Shelton. If they're both covered, Simpson you take the shot. That's it! Go!"

The boys throw down their towels, and Sweet gets the ball from the referee. The whistle sounds, and Sweet makes a clean in-bounds pass to Simpson. A Wolverine covers Simpson immediately, but Simpson manages to bounce-pass the ball to Shelton, who's 15 feet from the basket. He dribbles then shoots, but not before knocking over a defender. The ball hits the rim, rolls around the circumference, and drops in. The horn sounds, and the game is over. Three hundred people scream, then moan, then howl in unison, as through your leaping players you see the referee wave away the shot because of offensive charging. The basket is disallowed. Your players stand stunned, while the Wolverines pile onto each other.

You gather your team together in a quick huddle; some of them are teary-eyed. They're all exhausted. "It was close," you say. "We did as well as we could, and we have nothing to be ashamed of. They're a good team, and they beat us. Hold your heads high and shake their hands."

After the team members shake the hands of their opponents, you follow them toward the locker room amid a cacophony of booing, yelling, and crying. At the edge of the court, a man of about 40 whom you recognize as Frank Sweet's father is in the face of the referee. He's yelling and cursing at him and jabbing his forefinger at the referee's chest. The referee, slightly bigger than Mr. Sweet, is backpedaling a bit but otherwise does not respond.

You'd like to get into the locker room as quickly as possible. You could go around the two men on your way off the court. It's not really your fight, and in any case you don't want to stir up any trouble with the parent of one of your players. But you also happen to agree with the ref's call: Shelton did charge, and the basket shouldn't have been allowed. Still . . .

YOU'RE THE COACH!

WHAT WOULD YOU DO?

Think about the situation as if you were there yourself, particularly in terms of the **adult role models** asset. **How would you set a good example while not making the situation worse?** How would you handle the situation in a way that would promote assets and make a positive impact?

You walk over to the two men and put your arm around the aggressor. "Mr. Sweet," you say, "let it go. It was charging. We lost."

Mr. Sweet throws your arm off and spins around. "Don't you tell me it was charging! You made enough boneheaded calls to disqualify yourself from any say in this at all! The guy has to be planted there for a foul! He wasn't planted!"

"Mr. Sweet . . ."

And then Mr. Sweet starts jabbing his forefinger at *you*. You're keenly aware that your players are watching, and, strangely enough, you feel more pressure now than you did in the last timeout of the game.

"Mr. Sweet . . ."

"Don't soft-soap this, and don't give me any of your crap about the 'best team won'! If you're a man, you stand up against being robbed! And we were robbed!"

You look directly into Mr. Sweet's eyes, focusing intently. "Mr. Sweet," you say evenly, "if you want to discuss this, we can talk about it later. Right now, I have a team to take care of."

You turn away, hoping that the man doesn't take a swing at you. Your players, all except Frank Sweet, are staring at you; Frank is looking at the ground. You lead them into the locker room.

After showers, you debrief your players on the game. They're good kids, and they've taken the loss as well as can be expected.

During a lull, Frank Sweet speaks up: "Don't let my dad get to you, Coach. That's just the way he is sometimes. He's really a good guy."

"I would've knocked him flat," says Ron Shelton, and turns to Frank. "Sorry, man, but if he was in my face like that . . ."

You let them discuss what each of them would have done, should have done. You're content that you *showed* them what you would have done.

(For a letter you can use to help avoid a situation similar to this one, see *Pass It On at School! Activity Handouts for Creating Caring Schools* by Jeanne Engelmann, Activity Handout #67—Rules to Play By—For Parents Only.)

SITUATION 5: THE PARENTS WITHOUT A COMMUNITY

* * *

Soccer practice

Magnolia Soccer League

East Rutherford, Washington

Asset 3—Other adult relationships

Asset 13—Neighborhood boundaries

You can't help but smile as you watch Mike, your assistant coach, play "Red Light, Green Light" with the team. Ten-year-old boys are great—so much energy, so much love of fun, so much lack of guile. Mike whips around, shouts "Red light!," and Joseph screams with glee as he attempts to stop the soccer ball he's been dribbling and falls over in the attempt.

You really like all 10 boys in your group, but strangely enough, although everyone lives within two miles of each other, no one seems to have met each other before. You noticed the silence at the first practice, when you reviewed the procedures with individual parents as they dropped off their children. Everyone was polite, but there were no greetings of recognition. Now, it's two practices later, and the first game is a week and a half away. You still don't sense any community among the parents, and, now that you think of it, not a whole lot among the players, either. When you asked each player what school he went to, you got six different responses—three public schools, two private schools, and one special program for advanced learners. Even the players who go to the same school are in different classrooms.

"Is this a problem?" Mike asks over coffee after the day's practice. "Everyone seems to like each other enough, and the kids are playing well as a team. They don't have to be best buddies. They may not see much of each other after the season ends."

"No, they might," you counter. "They do live in the same neighborhood, after all."

"I guess so," says Mike. "Still, what's the problem?"

You wonder about that. Mike's right: they *are* playing well as a team—passing the ball instead of hogging it, complimenting each other after good plays, consoling each other after bad ones. You couldn't ask for more on-the-field camaraderie.

"What about after the game?" you ask Mike.

"After the game?"

The problem finally gels in your mind. "After each practice, everyone gets picked up and just, I don't know, goes away. What's going to happen during the games? Every parent will be rooting for the team as well as his or her own child, but will they be rooting for the other players as well?"

"Probably."

"Probably? I don't think so, Mike. I'm not sure they can even identify the other players. How can they yell, 'Nice block, Gage,' when they don't even know who Gage is?"

"Again, is this a problem?"

You sip your coffee. In the grand scheme of things, it's not a problem, you suppose. Parents aren't required to know all their children's teammates. It probably doesn't help the team win or lose. And no one is complaining about conflicts between the teammates.

You lift your mug to your lips and you notice your whistle dangling below: "IT'S ABOUT THEM." You think, and just for a moment, you lift yourself out of the context of a soccer league and you think about the kids as kids, not as players.

"It's a problem," you say to Mike. "I'm going to call a meeting. But before we have that meeting, you and I have some work to do."

YOU'RE THE COACH!

WHAT WOULD YOU DO?

Think about the situation as if you were there yourself, particularly in terms of the **other adult relationships** and **neighborhood boundaries** assets. **How would you form closer relationships among the parents and young people on your team without making it seem forced?** How would you handle the situation in a way that would promote assets and make a positive impact?

It's 6:30 in the evening, and everyone is gathered at the field. You know that the parents want to get this over with as soon as possible and return to their homes. It's the first thing you mention.

"Thank you for coming. I know you want to make this quick, and so do I. I'll try to have us out of here by 7:00. I think we have at least one parent of every player here, so again, thank you.

"First of all, the team is looking great. Your boys are wonderful. Even in the past couple of weeks, they've improved a lot—dribbling, shooting, blocking. Passing we still have to work on. More important, though, they're having fun, and I hope they're conveying that to you after practice. By now, I've gotten to know each player a little, and as you might expect, all kinds of personalities and abilities are represented, but this I can say: they're a fantastic team.

"A great team deserves lots of support, and I hope as many of you as possible will be coming out to the games, beginning this Saturday at 10:00, and cheering for us.

"That's what I want to talk to you about. It's easy to cheer for the team as a whole, and it's *very* easy to cheer for your own son, but I'd like to create more community than that.

"It struck me recently that although everyone lives fairly close to one another, no one seems to know each other. I wanted to provide an opportunity for us to get to know each other better, so that we really become a team. When the soccer season ends, I'm hoping our friendships might continue.

"You've all received team rosters, with everyone's name, address, and phone number. Mike will now pass out some more information. In each folder you receive are 'profiles' of two other boys on the team. We took photographs of the boys this week. Thank you again for signing the releases during registration. Those photographs are included. You also have lists of what those boys say are their interests outside soccer, and you have lists of what Coach Mike and I perceive are each boy's soccer-playing strengths.

"I'd like you to 'adopt' these boys. What does that mean? Greet them by name, and ask how they're doing. Cheer them on. Maybe if your son is interested, you can arrange for your families to get together sometime outside soccer. You're not limited to doing this with the boys whose information you received, but I'd like to make sure that all the kids have at least a couple of adults besides their parents to treat them special. Mike and I are making the same effort to get to know you and your boys. What I hope to see out of this season is not only good soccer but also kids who feel that there are a lot of adults who care about them. This should all be genuine. Don't think of what I'm asking you to do as an assignment. Think of it as a way to make everyone feel more of a team. Any questions?"

The meeting, you think, goes well. One parent even stands up during the discussion to formally express her appreciation for your efforts. In the end, you don't expect every adult to follow through, but you also figure that effort is a plus. The final indication that you're on the right track comes just as the last parent leaves. Mike comes up to you and says, "You know, this was a good idea."

SITUATION 6: DOING THE SPLITS

* * *

Gymnastics office

Meadowbrook Middle School

Bethlehem, New York

Asset 5—Caring school climate

Asset 6—Parent involvement in schooling

Margaret Clowder is very well-dressed—dark suit, sensible but expensive shoes—she's accessorized for power more than fashion. You think, lawyer? corporate executive? It turns out that she's very well-spoken, too. She doesn't smile, she doesn't waste words, and she has a level gaze that meets yours with ease. She sits across your desk at 9:00 on a Tuesday morning, and says she's come to see you about her daughter, Phaedra. Immediately, you feel defensive, and you're not sure why: Phaedra is doing quite well in your afterschool class and in her gymnastics tournaments.

"Phaedra is doing quite well in the class and in tournaments," you say, smiling, trying to defuse any anticipated attack.

"I'm sure she is," says Ms. Clowder. "I'm not here because I'm concerned about Phaedra's gymnastic performance."

"Okay," you say cautiously. "What can I help you with then?"

"My daughter is in the eighth grade this year; she'll be attending high school next year. I'd hoped to get her into the accelerated program at the high school. Until this year she was getting straight A's."

Now you have an inkling about what's coming. Phaedra is a very bright girl, definitely oriented toward achievement. She approached gymnastics warily at first, but then she threw herself into it with abandon.

"That doesn't surprise me," you say. "Phaedra is very smart, very studious."

"Ah," says Ms. Clowder, "'studious.' Well, you see, Phaedra is a lot less studious than she has been. These days, Phaedra is much more interested in splits and tumbling than math and science."

"Her grades have dropped?"

"Yes, her grades have dropped, and her priorities as well. Instead of doing the very best homework projects she can, now she's doing the very best back flips she can. I understand you advised her to keep a sock beneath her chin."

"It's to keep her head tucked in on back flips."

"No doubt. But Phaedra is convinced that she will never perform a correct back flip, so she practices it constantly. Aside from detracting from her studies, I'm not sure it's the most healthful thing she could be doing with her body."

You lean forward. Ms. Clowder has neither raised her voice nor shown any expression of tension on her face, but you can tell that she's dead serious about this, and you want to show her that you don't take this lightly, either.

"Ms. Clowder. First of all, let me assure you that we're very careful with what we do in gymnastics. Obviously, nothing is foolproof, but we're very good about taking precautions. Second of all, I hear what you're saying: you're concerned that Phaedra is neglecting her academics for gymnastics. I believe that both are important to Phaedra, but at this time of her life she's apparently concentrating on the gymnastics. What would you like me to do?"

Ms. Clowder leans forward in her chair, and the distance between you a minute ago has been cut in half.

"I've already talked to Phaedra about this, but obviously I've had little effect. For now, she seems to value your opinions more than her father's or mine. So I'm not going to tell you what to do. I'll just tell you what I've told Phaedra: school is for learning; participation in athletics is secondary. If her grades don't markedly improve by next month, then she is not to participate in gymnastics or any other athletic event until her grades do improve. I'm telling this to you so you know what is likely to happen."

Ms. Clowder gets up to leave, and you stand.

"Thank you for telling me," you say. You hold out your hand, and Ms. Clowder takes it.

"You're welcome."

Ms. Clowder walks out of your office, and you drop back in your chair. Once again, you're cognizant of what's written on your whistle: "IT'S ABOUT THEM." So it is about them, in this case Phaedra. Where do your interests lie? Are they always with the students? Are they always with the parents?

YOU'RE THE COACH!

WHAT WOULD YOU DO?

Think about the situation as if you were there yourself, particularly in terms of the **caring school climate** and **parent involvement in schooling** assets. **How would you respect both Phaedra's and her mother's opinions? Is it up to you or the parents to take the lead, or should you just leave it to Phaedra?** How would you handle the situation in a way that would promote assets and make a positive impact?

Three days after your meeting with Ms. Clowder, you call Phaedra into your office. You can't help but notice the similarities between the woman and the girl: the set gaze, the confident bearing, the no-nonsense conversation. You sit across from her and tell her what she already knows, that her mother will remove her from gymnastics unless her grades improve. You ask her what she thinks about this, and she says that, essentially, whatever will happen will happen.

"I want to offer you a plan," you say. "I've thought about this a lot. I'd like you to stay with gymnastics and I'd like you to improve your grades, too. But the only thing I can do is to present you with a way to do that and offer you encouragement. The rest is up to you. Are you interested?"

Phaedra says yes, and you give her the plan, telling her it's called the "SPLITS." She grins just a bit.

SPLITS

Schedule. Set up a schedule that allows for both athletics and academics.

Partner. Find partners to help you study. Try to get a friend to be one partner and a family member to be another.

Learning. Be sure that you're learning something, not just studying and memorizing.

Integration. Integrate this plan into your life, so you can still include special events, down times, and unforeseen circumstances.

Testing. Look at test scores, grades, and the effects on your life in general to determine whether the plan is working and how it might be adjusted.

Satisfaction. Don't try to follow through with the plan until you're satisfied with it; it has to work for *you* before it works for anyone else.

"What do you think?" you ask Phaedra after she looks it over.

Phaedra shrugs. "Makes sense," she says.

"It's not that easy," you say.

"I know."

"And you've got to do it for *you*."

"I know."

"Any questions before we get into this with a little more detail? We have a lot of work to do. We have to set up the schedule and identify some partners for you, we've got to figure out ways that you can enjoy yourself while studying, we have to figure out which grades to look at—why are you smiling?"

"Is this my plan or yours?"

Now you smile. "Sorry, I got carried away."

Phaedra's laugh is even rarer than her smile. "Why did you do this? Didn't you think that I'd be able to pick up my grades?"

"I didn't know. But I care about you whether you're on my team or not, so I thought I'd give it a shot. And it's tough to commit to both athletics and academics."

Phaedra nods. "Thanks," she says. "That's nice."

HUDDLE

INSTANT REPLAY

THE PROBLEM	THE ASSET-BUILDING SOLUTION
An angry parent accosts a referee after the game.	• Help build asset 14, adult role models. • Stay calm and show your players that you're able to avoid a potentially violent situation.
Players' parents don't know each other—there isn't much team "community."	• Help build asset 3, other adult relationships, and asset 13, neighborhood boundaries. • Provide parents with information about other players' skills and interests. Encourage them to bond with other team members.
A parent is upset that her daughter's grades are dropping.	• Help build asset 5, caring school climate, and asset 6, parent involvement in schooling. • Work with your player to create a plan to improve her academic performance.

Asset Referee: Questions?

Asset-Building Coach: *Well, at issue in the first situation obviously is what to do if the guy at the basketball game keeps coming at me. At some point, don't I have to defend myself?*

AR: Yes, but how best do you do that?

ABC: *I have to judge each situation as it comes up, don't I? All these situations are like that, aren't they?*

AR: Pretty much. There are some guidelines, but every situation is different. If the parent had come after you with fists flying, then yes, you would certainly have to protect yourself. But I think the situation you encountered would be more typical. *Not* fighting, even when provoked, is an excellent message to send to students. That's what being a role model is.

ABC: *I have a question about parents in general. Part of it is based on the soccer league situation, but it also has a lot to do with assets. It's all very fine to say, "Let's get all the parents to look after all the kids." And it's fine to say that adults should be role models. But honestly, some adults really aren't good role models. The guy at the basketball game is one example. Suppose you had some parents on the soccer team who were heavy drinkers or smokers, or vulgar, or violent. You wouldn't really want them taking an interest in the kids.*

AR: No, of course not. There are always exceptions. That's why what's on the whistle is so important: This is about *them,* the young people in your care. If it's not to a player's advantage to have a particular adult be close, then don't encourage that. I'll give you another example. Suppose that you had a parent who was a perfectly good role model but who didn't *want* to take an interest in other people's children? Would you force that parent to go along with your program and "bond" with a player? Of course not—because it wouldn't be to your player's advantage.

ABC: *I can easily relate to the last situation; the issue of time spent on sports as opposed to school is a very real one. Leaving the decision up to the student isn't always so effective, though. Sometimes the student* doesn't *know best. What student would prefer to study as opposed to play ball?*

AR: What student would prefer to flunk out as opposed to learning *and* playing ball?

ABC: *So I have to get that across to my students.*

AR: You have to respect the family. When Phaedra Clowder's mother came to you complaining about her daughter's grades, you didn't accept the fact that it would have to be either grades *or* gymnastics. You focused on a way to combine both of Phaedra's interests and strengths. That's what you have to do—be positive and find compromises—within the parameters of the family.

ABC: *It's not that easy.*

AR: You'll find that you have more control over promoting external assets than internal ones. It's a lot easier to control what *you* do, for example, than what your students do.

ABC: *Great.*

AR: Don't worry. You're doing fine. In the next three situations, you'll be working with communities, which are big and sometimes ungainly external environments. You'll try to figure out what to do when a community doesn't appreciate your athletes, when your athletes travel to a *new* community, and when a community threatens your athletes. Remember your whistle, and let's go!

THIRD 3 PERIOD

COMMUNITIES

SITUATION 7: NO FANS IN THE STANDS

* * *

Track & field meet

Northwest Middle School

Lansbury, Florida

Asset 4—Caring neighborhood

Asset 7—Community values youth

You can see it on the girls' faces—elation and disappointment at the same time. They congratulate each other on their wins—in the long jump and the 100-meter—and on their second- and third-place finishes in a few other events. But the joy is tinged with a hint of sadness.

"I am very proud of you girls," you say at the post-meet team gathering. "Joanna, great running. Cynthia, Kai, Daleesha, Robin, you have improved so much in the past month; nice finishes for all of you. And the big surprise—Noelle." Noelle looks directly at you, as usual, so she can read your lips. But you also sign to her, "You'll have something to tell your friends about tomorrow!"

"I wouldn't have to if they were here," signs Noelle back, and you communicate that to the others as they nod.

"Yeah," says Daleesha. "How many people were here from Northwest besides us and our families, Coach? Five? Six?"

Everyone starts to name and count off the people from the school who showed up for the meet. The number stops at eight.

"It's nice weather," you say feebly. "People have other things to do."

"It's not fair," signs Noelle. "People show up at football games. They go to basketball games."

"I've seen more people from school show up at bake sales," adds Robin.

"Maybe they don't know about our meets," suggests Joanna. "Maybe we need to publicize them more."

"They know about them," says Daleesha. "They're listed in the school paper. I know I told *my* friends to come."

"What did they say?" you ask.

"They shrugged me off and changed the subject. On Monday, they'll tell me about how they did something else that was so much more important than coming to the meet."

"Did you see how many people were cheering that girl from Roosevelt?" signs Noelle. "That probably gave her five more seconds on me. And it's our home turf!"

"When is our next home meet?" asks Joanna.

"In three weeks," you say. "And I want us to do something about this before then."

YOU'RE THE COACH!

WHAT WOULD YOU DO?

Think about the situation as if you were there yourself, particularly in terms of the **caring neighborhood** and **community values youth** assets. **How would you help your athletes generate community enthusiasm for their efforts?** How would you handle the situation in a way that would promote assets and make a positive impact?

"Lansbury isn't all *that* big a place," you say. "I cannot imagine why people in our town wouldn't want to come out and see you girls run your tails off. I have to believe that a 400-meter run is every bit as exciting as any given minute of a basketball game."

The girls laugh. Joanna says, "People in this town just don't have any experience with track & field, that's all."

"Then I think we should give them that experience," you say. "Take your showers. Then you can tell your families that I'm treating you all to pizza tonight."

Over pepperoni and vegetarian pizzas, salads, and sodas, you lay out your idea: to blanket Lansbury with notices about the upcoming track & field meet. "Now," you say, "how do we go about doing it?"

You've never seen the girls so excited. Kai immediately talks about making posters and placing them in the windows of local businesses. Robin thinks she knows someone whose mother works for the local radio station. Noelle wants to compose cheers, make copies of them, and hand them out on street corners. Robin suggests posting them in the library and the grocery stores.

Daleesha takes charge with a pen and a napkin and assigns responsibilities. Only Cynthia is quiet.

"Cynthia?" you ask. "Something wrong?"

"I think people will need more of a reason to go."

"What do you mean?" asks Daleesha. "Maybe I high-jump six feet and break a record. Isn't that reason enough?"

"Yeah," adds Robin. "What more do we have to do?"

"I think we should pay them."

This idea, of course, is met with loud denials and expressions of disbelief. But Cynthia is a strong-willed girl, and when everyone has finished pooh-poohing her suggestion, she continues.

"Let's ask some businesses, like this place"—she waves a hand around—"to give out, I don't know, discount coupons to anyone who goes to our meet. It's not a big deal. When Kai puts up the posters, she can add a second poster advertising the discount. Then we get businesses to agree to do it. We can go to the hamburger places, the cleaners, stores in the mall—all over."

"That's a great idea!" says Robin. "Girl, you are smarter than I gave you credit for!"

And, in a way, so are all of them—smarter than you gave them credit for. You set the stage for them to step up to a challenge. You'll help them along the way, but this is mostly their idea. And, you realize, that's what building assets is all about.

SITUATION 8: AWAY FROM HOME

* * *

Swim meet trip

Seward High School

Tumplut, Alaska

Asset 11—Family boundaries

You think to yourself that after being married to someone for 13 years, you'd know all that person's expressions, but this look of amazed incredulity is truly a new one.

"Let me get this straight: You're going to take 10 teenage boys—some of whom have never been more than five miles from home—on a plane to Seattle, a city of, what, half a million people? You're going to take them on this swim meet for three days—and, I might add, for three nights—with only one other adult to supervise them? Is that about right?"

It sounded better a minute ago, but the facts are all there.

"That's right, except it'll be only two nights. Three days and two nights. Good idea, huh?"

You ignore the shaking of her head and begin planning.

Later, you meet with Tony, your assistant coach.

"What do you think? Are we biting off more than we can chew?" you ask.

"Do you mean, should we have more chaperones?"

"Well . . ."

"Our budget won't handle any more adults. Besides, if we don't give young people responsibility, they'll never learn."

You agree with all that, but you're still feeling a little daunted.

"I know we're going to have rules," you say. "But I'm still a little uncomfortable about everything. Think of the temptations. There are strangers on the street and bars and . . ."

"Hey, hey!" laughs Tony. "We're just going to Seattle. The boys will be swimming all day. They'll probably be so tired when they get back to the hotel, they'll barely be able to stay awake after dinner."

"I know," you say. "They're all good kids. They're not the types to get in trouble. I know their parents and families. I'd just like a little more clout once we're there."

"You don't think our rules and our presence will be enough?"

You look Tony in the eye. "I wish it were," you say. "But I also wish we had some reinforcements."

YOU'RE THE COACH!

WHAT WOULD YOU DO?

Think about the situation as if you were there yourself, particularly in terms of the **family boundaries** asset. **How would you set rules that your students would respect?** How would you handle the situation in a way that would promote assets and make a positive impact?

You think about reinforcements all the time you're making out your Code of Conduct—the rules you want your students to follow and the consequences of breaking those rules. The code addresses issues such as when you expect them to be in their rooms at night, how much money they can carry, how they should behave with strangers, what they can and can't do by themselves, and of course prohibitions on smoking and drinking. These boundaries are probably what their parents would expect, anyway.

And of course that's your reinforcement.

You call up several of the parents and ask them to help you draft the Code of Conduct. After you've received their help, you think of an even greater reinforcement.

You and Tony take the Code of Conduct directly to the students.

"This is what some of your parents, Coach Tony, and I have drawn up. Look it over, see if you want to make any changes, add or take away some things. I can't promise we'll do what you say, but we'll certainly listen."

The students eagerly review the code and discuss it with animation. You and Tony walk out of the room while the discussion goes on and return in 15 minutes. You begin by saying that any family rule stricter than a team rule comes first for that individual. You also say that you want parents to review what the team determines is the final code. With that, you listen to the students' ideas.

They have two suggestions. First, they find the rule of being in the presence of a coach or a teammate at all times impractical and untrusting. Second, they believe that the coaches should have rules to govern them, too.

Another discussion ensues—a good-natured one at that. You and Tony decide to relent a little on the rule about always being with a coach or teammate, but you explain the rationale for the rule and make a deal with the team. You won't hold them to the letter of the rule if they obey its spirit, attempting to be with someone else if possible.

The team's second suggestion is almost embarrassing. "You're absolutely right," you say. "Coach Tony and I should have rules, too, and we will draw those up and present them to you. Thank you for that suggestion. Thank you for all the suggestions."

You revise the code and again ask for parents' input, which this time is minimal. Now you feel that you have the proper reinforcement. Parents have helped to make the rules consistent with their own, and the swimmers have a stake in the rules because they've had an opportunity to shape them. You've even added a few rules about the coaches' curfews (one hour later than the students'), smoking and drinking (none), and behavior toward the team (respectful and always giving them the benefit of the doubt).

Now you're looking forward to the trip.

SITUATION 9: WALKING HOME

* * *

Carling Bassett Tennis Club

Lake Honour, Ontario

Asset 10—Safety

Cool. Crisp. Leaves are starting to turn. It's a perfect day for tennis, you think. The thwacks of the balls being served and volleyed heighten the stillness of this pristine afternoon. You walk back and forth among the courts, commenting on Susan's arch before serving, on Rhonda's footwork when she goes for her backhand, on Ahn's grip. Just before 6:00, you bring the girls together for some last-minute instruction and then release them to their rides home. As you're gathering the balls, you can hear the girls saying their good-byes.

You begin what has become your favorite part of the day—the 40-minute walk home. This is your main time for exercise, but it's also a good opportunity to collect your thoughts. You think about the work you need to do when you get home and resolve to get to bed before 11:00.

It's over the morning paper that you almost scald yourself on your tea: "Girl Accosted in Bankhead Neighborhood." That's *your* neighborhood, and you hurriedly read the first paragraph: "A local girl, 14, was approached by a stranger yesterday evening while walking to her home. The stranger attempted to entice the girl to his car, but she ran to a nearby house. The girl said the man who approached her was about 5'10" with light features and a slender build. The girl's identity is being withheld."

Was it one of *your* girls? You'd thought that everyone had a ride, but you couldn't be sure—you were busy collecting equipment. Might one of the girls have decided to walk home?

You begin to make phone calls and, one by one, check off each girl's name. You can get to only about half before you have to leave for school. Not until after lunch are you finally certain that it wasn't one of your girls who was accosted.

What can you do after tennis practice is over? You can't be with the girls 24 hours a day. You can't hold practice earlier in the day, and weekend practice is just not enough for the girls to improve their skills.

The girl who was approached by a stranger was not on your team, but she easily might have been.

YOU'RE THE COACH!

WHAT WOULD YOU DO?

Think about the situation as if you were there yourself, particularly in terms of the **safety** asset. **How would you protect your students without interfering in their private lives?** How would you handle the situation in a way that would promote assets and make a positive impact?

In your office at school, you e-mail the parents of your team members. "Nothing is more important than the safety of your children," you write. "I want to set up a system that will account for all of our girls. If you don't pick up your girls after practice, then please let me know, and I'll arrange another way for your child to get home safely."

Not all the parents have e-mail, but you call and leave messages for those who don't. Over the next few days, only a few parents respond, and you realize that you should have asked them to respond to your message—whether or not they pick up their daughters. So once again, you call.

The results surprise you. Out of 14 girls on the team, nine are picked up and five walk home. Out of those five, two parents are willing to change their schedules to pick up their daughters or else arrange for a ride.

But three aren't. "It's only four blocks," says one. "She can take care of herself," says another. And the third gives no reason at all.

You're flabbergasted. You can't believe that parents aren't more concerned about their children's safety. Maybe you're overconcerned. Should you just drop the matter? Should you defer to the wishes of the parents?

> Again, think about the situation. Have your actions ensured the safety of your players? What would you do?

You bring out a map. One girl walks four blocks, another walks three blocks in a different direction, and a third walks two blocks in somewhat the same direction as the first girl. Theoretically, the first and third girls could walk together, but that would still leave the first girl walking alone for part of the time. The second girl would clearly be on her own.

You gaze down at the map and yet again notice your whistle: "IT'S ABOUT THEM." You shake your head and realize that the solution is quite simple. You fold up the map and make three phone calls.

You tell the parents that if it's okay with them, you'll drive the three girls home. The parents don't have to do anything different, and the girls will be warmer in your car than they would be if they walked home. You don't tell the parents that you're giving up your exercise, your alone time, and your pride at not fouling the Lake Honour air with your car's exhaust during the week.

The remaining parents agree—begrudgingly, you think. You finger your whistle as a parent tells you, "If you insist." You realize that you won't always be there to shelter the girls on your team.

But as long as you're their coach, you will.

HUDDLE

INSTANT REPLAY

THE PROBLEM	THE ASSET-BUILDING SOLUTION
Your team generates little enthusiasm for their meets.	• Help build asset 4, caring neighborhood, and asset 7, community values youth. • Empower team members to develop strategies for improving attendance, such as partnering with local businesses to offer discount coupons for attending meets or games.
You're worried that an out-of-town sports event will be dangerous for the players.	• Help build asset 11, family boundaries. • Work with parents to determine what boundaries and consequences are needed and appropriate. Ask students for their input as well.
Students may not be safe walking home from practice.	• Help build asset 10, safety. • Check with parents to see whether they are arranging rides for their children. Consider driving students yourself.

Asset-Building Coach: *I have one big question about these situations.*

Asset Referee: Let's hear it.

ABC: *It seems to me that what distinguishes the Developmental Assets framework is its emphasis on young people's strengths, as opposed to their weaknesses.*

AR: Yes, that's accurate.

ABC: *When I got the girls excited about publicizing their track meet, I was playing to their strengths. I can see that. But in the other examples—*

setting up guidelines for the trip to Seattle, driving the girls home after tennis, I don't know. I felt that I was just solving problems, and I'm not even sure that they were genuine problems. In any case, anyone could have handled the situations, even someone who didn't know anything about Developmental Assets.

AR: That sounds like two questions. Let me first answer the one about solving problems, and then we'll talk about whether something is a genuine problem. While it's true that others may have chosen to do what you did, they may not have been aware of why they chose well. And, explicitly or not, you helped promote assets with every one of your responses to the situations.

Sometimes asset building *is* "just solving problems," and there's nothing wrong with that. There are many effective ways to solve problems, but not all of those ways will promote assets.

Not every problem has a solution that leaves a positive impact on young people. You may have "only" responded to a problem of little fan support with the girls on your track team, but look at the outcome! They worked together on a project and gained valuable skills and insights. They drew closer to their community. So even if not one extra person showed up at the next meet, which is extremely unlikely, they would have benefited immensely. With the Alaskan swim team, you faltered a little by drawing up a Code of Conduct without your students' initial contributions, but you recovered by taking it to them afterward. And you had a very difficult situation with the Canadian tennis families. Sometimes you're left with what may appear to be an unsatisfactory solution to a problem. But in this case you chose wisely; the safety of your students was paramount. And the actual asset—safety—was undoubtedly promoted as well. Could someone with no knowledge of Developmental Assets have done all this? Possibly. But your knowledge of the assets provided you with a framework—a direction to solve the problems—that's an enormous advantage.

ABC: *But I'm not even sure that the field trip to Seattle was a problem at all. They may have done just fine without my intervention.*

AR: I'm glad you brought that up. Think about your role as coach. Do you teach your players the rules of the game and then simply let them play without further coaching? Do you wait until they make a mistake before you give them additional information and teach them new skills? No, of course not. This situation is similar.

ABC: *I guess that's true. It doesn't matter if the situation is home or away. If I can help students become more comfortable within their communities, then I've done a pretty good job as a coach.*

AR: And if you can help students become more comfortable with their *society,* then you've done a *great* job as a coach. The next three situations address societal issues—sexism, drugs, and control. Speaking of control, as you tackle more complex issues, you'll find that you have less of it.

ABC: *I'm ready.*

FOURTH 4 PERIOD

SOCIETY

SITUATION 10: PLAYING "LIKE GIRLS"

* * *

Post-basketball game

Lincoln High School

Chicago, Illinois

Asset 27—Equality and social justice

Asset 34—Cultural competence

"The Loggers rule!"

"Go, Loggers! Go, Loggers! Go, Loggers!"

You're not yelling and grunting and punching the boys on their shoulders, but you have to admit that it's pretty exciting beating a team that's favored to beat *you* by 15 points.

"Who's Number 1! Who's Number 1!"

You smile at your players as they celebrate and shower and celebrate some more.

"They thought they could beat us! They were so sure they were better than us!"

"But they weren't!"

"No one can beat the Loggers!"

"They played like girls!"

"We're Number 1! We're Number 1!"

Long after the emotional evening, long after you turn out the light and settle into your bed, the comment gnaws at you like a termite on a plank. "They played like girls." In other words, they played poorly. No, the phrase doesn't imply that they just played poorly; playing poorly is when you don't execute. "Playing like girls" means you *can't* execute, because you lack the sufficient skills to do so. Oh well, you think, it's nothing, and you fall asleep thinking of all the great decisions you made to get the Loggers their well-deserved win.

You happen to have a faculty meeting on Monday afternoon, and afterward, over coffee, you ask Jim Phehan, the football coach, whether he thinks that high school girls could ever beat high school boys in a basketball game.

"Depends on the girls and the boys," says Jim reasonably.

"The best players of each," you say.

Jim thinks for a second. "No way," he says. "Boys are taller, stronger, faster, and quicker. They always will be."

"But not cleverer."

Jim smiles. "Not necessarily cleverer."

"It's not a fair comparison, is it," you say.

"Not really. What's on your mind?"

"One of my guys said that the Bears played like girls last Friday."

"Oh, come on, you're not going to get politically correct on me, are you?" asks Jim. "It's just a comment. He meant that they played bad. What's the big deal?"

You've had your differences with Jim before on a variety of social and political issues, but you respect his judgment.

"I don't know. I guess I *am* going to get politically correct on you. I understand what he meant, but I'm afraid the meaning is too general in their minds. Like, to 'play like a girl' means to play poorly. To do anything 'like a girl' means to do anything poorly."

"I think it's confined to athletics."

"I don't know. Even if it is, it seems demeaning to me. I think we have a responsibility to expunge that attitude, or at least make students aware of its consequences."

"Lighten up," says Jim. "Girls aren't built like boys, and as such, they have different capabilities. None of our guys can have babies. That doesn't make them inferior human beings."

"It's not the same thing," you say. "Boys don't aspire to have babies. Girls do aspire to play sports."

"But no girl was in the locker room to hear the comment, was she?"

You look at Jim and smile. He thinks you're smiling because you've accepted his arguments, but you're smiling because you've discarded them.

"So you wouldn't do anything at all?" you ask, already knowing the answer.

"Not a darn thing. And neither will you, unless you want to cause mass unconsciousness because your whole team rolls their eyes out of their sockets."

YOU'RE THE COACH!

WHAT WOULD YOU DO?

Think about the situation as if you were there yourself, particularly in terms of the **equality and social justice** and **cultural competence** assets. **How would you persuade your students that their attitudes about females are both inaccurate and disrespectful? Or are you being overly sensitive?** How would you handle the situation in a way that would promote assets and make a positive impact?

"Why are we staying in the locker room, Coach?" asks Lonnie Paul, one of your forwards.

"We're not going to practice today," you say. "We're going to watch another team practice."

Lonnie frowns and looks at his teammates, who have similar expressions.

"I want you all to stay in the locker room until I know the other team is in the gym. I'd rather take you out there once they've already started."

"What team are we going to see?"

"I'd like to save the answer to that for later."

"Hey, a mystery!" says one of your players. "Coach is having his family play out there, and he doesn't want them to be embarrassed."

Everyone laughs, and someone says, "Should we watch for anything special?"

"Everything," you say. "I want you to watch everything they do—shoot, dribble, block, pass. Maybe you'll pick up some pointers."

"This is going to be cool," says Lonnie.

Fifteen minutes later, you hear the familiar sounds of bouncing balls, short bursts of chatter, and occasional shouts of self-congratulation. You lead your boys out onto the bleachers and usher them all into the front row.

"These are girls!" says Carl Dawson, your center.

"They're the Passing Slammers," you say. "They're part of a local woman's league. I've seen them play before, and I think you can learn a lot from them."

You hear a groan or two and some sprinkled tittering, but that soon stops when one of the Slammers dribbles the ball the length of the court, evading a "defender" who's positioned at half-court. She pivots, spins, turns, switches the ball from hand to hand, feints, and barely makes her way past the other player. Then she returns to half-court, acting as the defender for the next player.

"Whoa," you hear from one of the boys, and you can't help smiling.

The next hour is more of the same. The Slammers go through defending, dribbling, passing, rebounding, and shooting drills. By the time they're through, the boys are cheering each outstanding move.

After a particularly strenuous drill in which one player deliberately bangs a shot off the backboard, two other players vie for the rebound, and the one who gets the rebound shoots, the manager of the Slammers approaches the bleachers.

"This is Judy Cambronne, boys," you say, "the Slammers' manager."

"Pleased to meet you," says Judy. "You had a pretty good game the other night. Any of you up for a little game right now?"

The boys accept eagerly, and you call on your five starters to take the court.

For the next half hour, you sub freely, as does Judy. You don't keep score, but the boys do. The final score is Slammers 28, Loggers 6.

"Good game, boys," says Judy, and the players from both teams shake hands and compliment each other's play.

In the clubhouse, the boys smile humbly.

"Man, we were whipped," says Lonnie Paul. "Twenty-eight to six? I hope no one hears about *this*."

"You played very well," you say. "They're professionals—or semi-professionals—anyway."

"They're awesome," says one of your boys. "They could have beat us 58 to 6 if they'd wanted to."

"Face it," says Carl Dawson. "We played like girls."

"No," says Lonnie Paul, quietly and with more than a tinge of admiration. "They did."

SITUATION 11: THE USERS

* * *

Baseball locker room

Southlawn High School

Los Angeles, California

Asset 31—Restraint

"Coach, I know you heard me talkin' about steroids. I ain't saying I'm taking 'em, and I ain't saying I ever *will* take 'em. All I'm saying is that you shouldn't go making like they're the devil or something, 'cause they ain't. Ballplayers take 'em all the time, and I don't see any ballplayers growing breasts, you understand what I'm saying?"

"I do understand, Rance, but I think you're mistaken about what steroids do and who takes them."

"Coach, I had health class. I know what they say. I also have a brother at State. He knows guys on the team, and I'm tellin' you,

Coach, they pop 'em like candy. And I don't think they stop poppin' 'em when they get to the bigs, understand?"

"So what are you telling me, Rance, that because you think that some ballplayers take steroids to enhance their performance, then it's a good idea?"

"Like I say, I'm just sayin', okay?"

You should be used to conversations like this one by now, you think, but you're not. You were playing the "Dirt" drill outside. You put a man on first, a man on second, and a man on third. You pitch to the catcher. Some balls you pitch well; others you deliberately throw poorly. If the catcher is going to miss the ball, everyone is supposed to yell "Dirt!" The runner on first is supposed to take off immediately, while the runners on second and third are supposed to take running leads to see how far away the ball is from the catcher before they decide whether to take the base. If they decide to run, then the catcher can try to throw them out.

This afternoon, Rance tried to go to third on an errant pitch and the catcher threw him out by three feet. Rather than question his judgment, Rance cursed his legs. "Man, I need more muscles!" he exclaimed bitterly. Hence, the discussion in the locker room with his teammates and then with you about steroids.

Linda McCutcheon is the girls' soccer and lacrosse coach. She knows what she'd do.

"I'd make sure that everyone knows exactly what's going to happen to them if they get caught with steroids: First, they're thrown off the team. Second, they're suspended from school. Third, they're in trouble with the law. And in case that's not enough, I'd tell them about the facial hair the girls will get, the baldness and breast development that the boys can expect, and the halted growth that will happen to each of them if they use steroids. No tolerance whatsoever."

"Linda, that's all well and good, but don't you think the students know that already?"

"Then they just don't have any excuse, do they."

"I think they believe that every athlete uses steroids."

"Irrelevant. Suppose every athlete drank their own urine and painted their navels purple."

"They'd probably do that, too, if they thought it would help."

"Doesn't anyone believe in reason anymore?"

You smile. "Like us?"

"See you later, Coach."

Rance is a popular kid, a good outfielder, and an excellent hitter. But you have to believe that what *he* believes is a minority opinion. Still, he probably carries more authority than you do with his peers. Maybe Linda is right. Maybe you have to set such stark boundaries and consequences for transgression that your players won't even be tempted to use steroids—or any other drug, for that matter.

YOU'RE THE COACH!

WHAT WOULD YOU DO?

Think about the situation as if you were there yourself, particularly in terms of the **restraint** asset. **How would you increase the probability that your athletes avoid using steroids? Is it a matter of laying down the law, or can you get them to use restraint voluntarily?** How would you handle the situation in a way that would promote assets and make a positive impact?

It's funny how often catching a glimpse of the whistle hanging from your neck makes you rethink ideas. If this issue really is "about them," then you have to look at it from their perspective. They've heard good and bad information about steroids. Maybe they believe what they've heard and maybe they don't.

Why would students decide to use steroids? Is it peer pressure? You don't think so. You think that peer pressure probably affects students' decisions to smoke or drink, but you don't think it works that way with steroids. You think that students might be tempted to use them to get an edge over their competitors. Are they trying to be like their perception of professional ballplayers?

Talking with Rance will do no good. He's already told you what he thinks, and he doesn't seem susceptible to your arguments.

But he might be susceptible to others'.

With that in mind, you call a team meeting.

"I'd like you boys to discuss steroid use," you say. "Not with me, but among yourselves. I'll be glad to answer questions, give you information, get you back on track if you stray, and so on. But I'd prefer just to listen. Talk about why you think using steroids might be a good idea, a bad idea, and so on. Nothing you say will leave this room, though I have to tell you that if I hear one of you admit to currently using steroids, then I have to refer that information to school authorities. But I want you to feel free to speak your honest opinions. Don't say what you think I want to hear. This is more for you than for me."

"Why are we doing this?" asks Zere, your second baseman.

"Well," you say, "I think that sometimes people act in ways they think their peer group approves of, even when they don't *know* what their peer group approves of. It's like everyone painting their navels purple because they think everyone else will think it's cool, when in fact no one thinks it's cool. So I'm giving you an opportunity to discover, out in the open, what each of you thinks about something important."

The discussion begins, and at first everyone is cognizant of your presence. But soon you seem to fade away from their consciousness, and they open up more. Rance and a few others lead the discussion, and it's difficult for you not to interfere, especially when they're giving out misinformation. Occasionally you notice a few students stealing glances at you for your reaction, but you try to remain stoic.

After about 10 minutes, something interesting happens. One or two students begin to speak up with opinions contrary to Rance's. They say that they, too, know some college athletes, and that none of them use steroids. They say that using steroids is stupid because the risks far outweigh the benefits. They say that even if they did get bigger muscles, they wouldn't want to mess up the rest of their body. Some of them also give out what you feel is misinformation, but, again, you hold back.

In half an hour, the tide has completely turned. Even Rance is retreating to the position that college ballplayers who use steroids are taking unnecessarily foolish risks. The consensus seems to be that using steroids is a bad idea.

You reenter the group and set them straight on a few facts—

some of the physiologic and psychologic effects, and the latest data about how many people actually do report using steroids (very few) and about students' opinions of those who do use steroids (very low). You thank them for the discussion, say you've learned a lot, and tell them that if they ever have any questions or comments about the use of steroids or any other drugs, you'll be glad to listen and to give them information.

After everyone has left, Rance approaches you, smiling.

"Hey, Coach, what'd I tell you?"

"Please, tell me again."

"I told you, Coach. Steroids aren't the devil or anything like that. Most of us wouldn't even go near that stuff. We're not dumb."

"No, you're not, Rance. Thanks for the opportunity to hear it straight from the horse's mouth."

"Hey, no prob', Coach. Anytime you want to know about anything else—sex, drugs, whatever—you just call another of these meetings, 'kay?"

"You'll be the first to know. Thank you."

"See ya, Coach."

You watch Rance leave the locker room and fervently hope that you don't hear him talking about sex anytime soon.

(For information about steroids, see page 110, The Truth about Steroids.)

SITUATION 12: IN CONTROL

* * *

Orientation

Li'l Spikers Volleyball League

Meadowlark, Wisconsin

Asset 32—Planning and decision making

Asset 37—Personal power

You've met all the new children and their parents. The routine went like this: The child and either the mother or father—rarely both—would enter the facility and find your office. The parent would introduce the child, and you'd say hi. Then you'd ask the child a few questions. "Have you ever played volleyball before?" "Where do you go to school?" "What's your favorite TV show?" Next you'd give the parent the paperwork—some forms to read and sign, others to read and take home. You'd answer any of the parents' questions. "What clothing do we need?" "Will there be breaks?" After about a total of 10 minutes, you'd say to the child, "See you on the 17th!" and parent and child would leave.

Granted, the children were only about 11 years old, but what struck you every time was how little they talked. Your experience has led you to believe that of every 12 kids, probably three don't want to be there and another three just don't care. Saturday mornings at 10:00, they'd rather be with their friends, watch TV, play an electronic game, or sleep in.

The season always turns out to be fun. Virtually all of the kids learn how to serve and return a volleyball, some learn how to spike, and a few even learn how to set. But the process starts here, and the kids usually form a bond with their teammates and enjoy the games. They even seem to have fun during the practice drills, such as using their serves to hit targets you've placed on the floor.

So what's missing? Why do you sometimes have the feeling that the league could be so much more beyond volleyball? You get that feeling again when you see the silent kids guided by their parents—the children following their parents' wishes, not necessarily their own.

Can you compel these young people to show initiative? You're the coach, of course, but it says "IT'S ABOUT THEM" on your whistle. What can you do to make this experience *the children's* experience?

YOU'RE THE COACH!

WHAT WOULD YOU DO?

Think about the situation as if you were there yourself, particularly in terms of the **planning and decision making** and **personal power** assets. **How would you give the young**

people control but not have the season devolve into chaos? How would you handle the situation in a way that would promote assets and make a positive impact?

As the children come onto the court, some hesitantly, you check the list you drew up over the past several days:

1. Name
2. Commitments
3. Recognition
4. Celebrations
5. Parents' day
6. Drills

You ask the children to sit in a circle with you, and for the next several minutes you introduce yourself, have them introduce themselves, and play a warm-up game.

Then you show everyone your whistle and point out that the words "IT'S ABOUT THEM" means exactly that. You say that you want this session to be a great experience for them. One way to do that is for them to be involved in that experience. And so you go down your list.

First you ask them to choose a team name. There's some crossover, but for the most part, the boys want "Rockets" and the girls want "Orioles." Eventually the group decides on "Wizards."

You tell them that in order for everyone to get the most out of the league, everyone needs to make a commitment to helping each other, supporting each other, and treating each other with respect. You ask them how they might do that, and you write their ideas on chart paper. Some of the commitments they suggest include:

- We'll listen to each other.
- We'll compliment each other on good plays.
- We'll apologize if we accidentally bump into someone.

- We'll pay attention to the coach.
- We'll be good sports.

You tell them that in the future they'll discuss what "good sports" means, but for now you congratulate them on coming up with some valuable commitments.

Next you say you'd like them to think of ways to recognize outstanding performance. You give the example of a weekly award for the person who makes the best shot or the one who improves the most. The children talk for a while and come up with the Wizard's Award, a certificate for the player who has the best overall performance for the day. Someone suggests giving awards at the end of the last day for those who have most improved.

You know that everyone is itching to play, so you end the discussion, noticing that to some extent it's helped them to bond with each other. As they play, they incorporate their commitments and compliment each other on good shots.

The next time you gather, you ask the players to think of ways to celebrate at the end of the sessions. You say that in addition to a celebration you'd like to have a "Parents' Day" to show their parents their new skills and accomplishments. You remind them that they each have a list of their teammates' phone numbers and that they can do some of the planning away from the facility.

Finally, you tell them that over the next few weeks you're going to be introducing them to a lot of different drills and practices. After they do each one once, you say that you'd like them to choose which one to do next.

During ensuing sessions, you check in with the players to see if they have any commitments they'd like to add to their list, to see if they have other ideas about recognitions or celebrations, and to check on their progress in planning Parents' Day. Eventually, they decide to include three things on Parents' Day: a highlight of some of the skills they've learned, a game, and an awards presentation. They also say that they'd like their parents to chip in and purchase Wizards T-shirts.

The sessions turn out to be the most enjoyable you've ever had. You even receive a surprise gift from the players: a "Best Volleyball Coach Ever" plaque. You know that because of their investment they are largely responsible for the success of the program.

But you do appreciate the plaque.

HUDDLE

INSTANT REPLAY

THE PROBLEM	THE ASSET-BUILDING SOLUTION
Your male players state that another team plays like girls.	• Help build asset 27, equality and social justice, and asset 34, cultural competence. • Expose your players to female athletes with tremendous talent.
A player praises the use of steroids.	• Help build asset 31, restraint. • Encourage a discussion about drug use among your players. Participate only to clarify misinformation.
Players seem to be participating more for their parents than for themselves.	• Help build asset 32, planning and decision making, and asset 37, personal power. • Give the players some control, such as determining how to celebrate at the end of the season and the order in which to do drills.

Asset-Building Coach: *I'm a little dissatisfied this time.*

Asset Referee: Why is that?

ABC: *I'm not sure that these situations are transferable. For instance, with the boys who thought girls couldn't play basketball well, I was able to get a local team to show the boys what women can do. But what if I lived in a part of the country where a local women's basketball team didn't exist? What would I have done then?*

AR: You probably would have been more creative. You may have found a videotape of a women's basketball game and played it for your team. You may have found one woman who played basketball, who could come in and show your students her talents. Or, if you found nothing relating to women's basketball, you may have chosen to feature women in another sport—softball or tennis. At the very least, you would have freed your students from the notion that women are incapable of high levels of achievement in sports.

ABC: *I also wonder about the strategy of letting the baseball team talk about steroid use. How did I know that the discussion would turn out to be positive?*

AR: You probably had a pretty good idea going in that most of your team wasn't in favor of using steroids. That would have been inconsistent with what attitude surveys tell us about youth. Think how much more powerful our attitudes are when we realize that we're in the majority. That's the beauty of this kind of strategy: If the anti-drug attitude is dominant—and it usually is—then that gives everyone a chance to see it. If by chance a minority of students have a strong pro-drug attitude, then this strategy hasn't cost you anything. The important thing for adults is to stay out of the discussion, except perhaps for correcting misinformation. If all it took to form young people's attitudes was for adults to tell them what to think, then we wouldn't be doing any of this.

ABC: *I guess that makes sense.*

AR: Any more questions?

ABC: *No, I guess not.*

AR: Don't you want to discuss anything about the children in the volleyball league?

ABC: *That situation seemed pretty standard, almost boring. I arranged for them to do some extra stuff to get them more involved and help them have more fun playing volleyball. I understand the importance of making the orientation of a volleyball league or a P.E. class student-centered. That can mean letting go of some control. As a result things might get a little messy.*

AR: Many coaches—and teachers—find letting go extremely difficult to do.

ABC: *Sure, but it still seemed like a no-brainer, at least in hindsight.*

I mean, if you hadn't given me this whistle, with the "IT'S ABOUT THEM" on it, I may not have found the energy to do what I eventually did. But I understand all that.

AR: Interesting. This is one of the most basic situations in the book—not standard—but basic. This type of situation is *fundamental.* When you come across a situation that doesn't cry out for attention—for example, when you're with a group of young people who don't seem to lack anything in particular—*that* is fertile ground for building assets.

Why? Because perceptive people can identify trouble, and dedicated and competent people can do something about it. But building assets isn't about identifying trouble and then doing something about it; it's about identifying *strengths* and doing something about *that.* When, without prompting, you took the initiative to give those young people the opportunity to identify and capitalize on their strengths, to show them that they had the resources to accomplish something—*that's* the essence of building assets.

ABC: *What do the next situations have in store?*

AR: Our next situations relate to individual attitudes—attitudes about nature and nurture, about action and inaction, and about winning and losing. Specific phrases are going to play an important part in each of these situations: "We're just girls." "You are so gay." And "It's my fault." Just remember, whatever the situation, remain positive. Look to the strengths.

FIFTH 5 PERIOD

ATTITUDES

SITUATION 13: THE CULTURE OF GIRLS

* * *

GirlSports sports camp

Mesa Costa Community Center

Point Alamar, California

Asset 16—High expectations

In the comfort of your own bed, after recovering from a hard day, you watch the 10:00 news. Featured is a story about a group of girls who climbed a mountain in Colorado. One of the people interviewed says with admiration, "And they're just girls!" You're reminded of what Maria said earlier.

It was near the end of the first day of the weeklong GirlSports sports camp, a potpourri of athletic activities spanning the spring break and intended to give preteen girls basic training in basketball, baseball, soccer, tennis, and golf.

You were having the girls get the feel of the basketball by circling the ball around their bodies, exchanging it from hand to hand—starting at the head and moving onto the midsection, the right leg, the left leg, through the legs, and finally reversing back to the head. You were explaining how important it was to retain control of the basketball in a game, and that the more comfortable they were with holding the basketball in both hands in various positions, the more likely they'd be able to retain control.

That was when Maria said it. She made the statement partly to the others, partly to you: "Heck, we don't care about being good in basketball, as long as we *look* good playing. We're just girls." You couldn't tell how many of the others agreed with her and how many didn't. Suffice it to say that at least a few nodded, smiled, and said, "Yeah."

And that troubles you.

That night you have a dream. All your girls are playing basketball, wearing gowns and heels. Their hair is bunned, and they're accessorized with earrings, necklaces, and bracelets. They pass the ball well, but they don't jump, lunge, or dribble. Everywhere you can hear the crowd murmuring, "They look really good out there."

In the morning, over breakfast, you make a list of what may be promoting such a defeatist self-image among the girls in your camp:

- Their families;
- Their friends;
- Their cultures; and
- Their experiences.

You take a deep breath and then make a list of what you might do to counter the self-image:

- Explain the benefits of being athletic (other than looking good);
- Get them to enjoy sports; and
- Convince them that they can do well in sports.

You look at the two lists and sigh again. You know which one you'd put money on. It's time to think about how you can turn their minds around in less than a week.

And then it comes to you. The plan isn't foolproof, and it's different from anything you've done before, but it's certainly worth a try. You get on the phone to call the other camp coaches.

YOU'RE THE COACH!

WHAT WOULD YOU DO?

Think about the situation as if you were there yourself, particularly in terms of the **high expectations** asset. **How would you convince Maria that, as both an individual and a girl, she has the potential to be athletic?** How would you handle the situation in a way that would promote assets and make a positive impact?

Tuesday is softball day. Typically, you'd have everyone do some exercises, explain the basic rules of the game, and divide the girls into rotating groups for batting, fielding grounders, and fielding flies. You'd end up with a makeshift game, in which everyone got to bat, run, and field.

Today, though, will not be a typical day. Today you begin with an assessment. You have each girl bat, field grounders, and field flies. Then you meet with your coaches and divide the girls into three squads—based not on their weaknesses but on their strengths. The girls who already bat pretty well get more practice hitting. The girls who field grounders well but are hesitant about fielding flies get more practice fielding grounders. And the girls who can position themselves well under fly balls—the smallest group—get even more practice shagging flies. Both fielding groups practice throwing as well.

You assign yourself to the batting group, which Maria is a part of. You let the girls take turns batting for a while—one girl batting, one girl pitching, and the rest fielding. As the morning progresses, you increase the specificity of your training. You show the girls the correct way to grip a bat, how to stand in the batter's box, and how to swing at the ball. You explain how to turn the shoulder, to move the hands, to shift weight, to rotate the hips, to keep the eyes level. By lunchtime, the girls, including Maria, have made much improvement. Where before they were hitting one out of four pitches, now they're hitting three out of four. Where before they were hitting grounders, now they're pounding out line drives.

More important, they're excited.

"Yes!" Maria punches the air with her fist as her last swing propels the ball into deep left-center field, where another group is hauling in flies.

During lunch, you compare notes with the other coaches. They have similar experiences to report. Girls are positioning themselves better for flies as well as grounders. They're throwing the ball more deliberately and on less of an arc. And they, like Maria, are excited at their progress.

Toward the end of the day, you rotate the groups, and surprise of surprises, the success they experienced in their "strong" area has carried over to their "weak" areas. The confidence they've gained transfers to the other facets of the game. The culminating game at 4:00 is competitive, exciting, and well played.

You make sure to say good-bye to Maria at the end of the day. "Soccer tomorrow," you say. "Any thoughts?"

"I wish we could play softball another day."

"But you're just a girl."

Maria smiles. "Just a girl who can smash monster home runs. I'll probably score a dozen goals tomorrow."

She turns to leave, then peeks back at you. "And look good doing it."

SITUATION 14: STANDING BY

* * *

Hallway

Pokela Elementary School

St. Paul, Minnesota

Asset 15—Positive peer influence

Asset 26—Caring

"You are so gay."

The statement resonates with you, hours after you heard it in the hallway. Ascribing "gayness" to someone doesn't have quite the same meaning as it did when you were younger, but it's close. When you're "gay," you're ineffectual and weak. Being "gay" is the antithesis of being cool.

And, like lions looking to pounce on the lame antelope, kids know the ones to zero in on. This time they've targeted Coby Larsen, a boy who's a little slower, a little less agile, and, yes, a little weaker than the others in your P.E. class. Yesterday was especially rough for Coby. You had your students climbing ropes, and poor Coby didn't have the upper-body strength to lift himself more than a foot or two above the ground.

What struck you about the hallway incident, though, was how many people just stood around when the epithet was hurled. You didn't see the perpetrator, but you saw Coby at his locker, with about five boys and girls standing around him—smiling, laughing, and adding derisive comments of their own. You know most of the students, and you're surprised that some of them would participate in such harassment. And by any definition, harassment is certainly what it was. This wasn't an offhand, lighthearted comment to be quickly thrown to the winds and wafted away; this was a direct insult to a boy who could ill-afford it. And you suspect that it's one in a sequence of hurtful remarks.

You regret not having interceded at the time, but you were already past the scene when the comment actually registered. You looked back, and the crowd around Coby's locker was beginning to disperse. These are 10-year-olds! They're numb to inflicting pain on others and to tolerating pain being inflicted on others. Someone wasn't getting mercilessly pummeled, but you feel this action lies along the same continuum.

You're the coach. In a way, you provide the environment in which these attitudes—of physical superiority and inferiority, of *moral* superiority and inferiority—often fester. Doesn't the "IT'S ABOUT THEM" on your whistle mean that not only is it your responsibility to quash those attitudes, but also, eventually, it's theirs?

YOU'RE THE COACH!

WHAT WOULD YOU DO?

Think about the situation as if you were there yourself, particularly in terms of the **positive peer influence** and **caring** assets. **How would you change the attitudes of your students so that it wouldn't seem authoritarian?** How would you handle the situation in a way that would promote assets and make a positive impact?

You decide to take a two-pronged approach. You have a good relationship with one of the boys in your class, Matt Dreaney. He's a natural leader, a good student, popular with his classmates, and deferential to adults but not slavish to authority. Your relationship with another student, Jacob Fine, isn't as good, but despite his predilection for getting into trouble and occasionally treating people with self-absorbed indifference, he is also considered a leader, probably because of his athletic prowess. You ask these two boys to meet with you because of their influence—positive *and* negative—on their peers.

"I need your help," you tell them. The three of you are sitting on the stands outside. There's a chill in the air, but the atmosphere is informal, which you think will offset the hierarchical relationship between you and the boys.

"More than many of your classmates," you say, "each of you is in a position to influence your friends. Students look up to you."

Based on their silent nods, you feel that you've got their attention—not so much, you think, because you've flattered them, but more because you've made them aware of how much responsibility they have.

"Lately," you continue, "I've been seeing a lot of . . . teasing going on—students calling other people names, making fun of people, stuff like that. To a certain point, joking around is fine. But when it's purposely hurtful, then I think that's wrong. What do you think?"

Both boys opine that most of the teasing they're seeing is harmless.

"That's good," you say. "But what if it's not harmless? What if someone is hurt by what someone else says or does?"

Matt says that he'd be against that. Jacob says he would, too.

"Good." you say. "We're in agreement. So here's what I'd like you to do. I want you to be not-so-innocent bystanders. When you see or hear something hurtful or mean going on, say something. Do something that will help the person being teased or bullied. Say, 'That's not cool,' or 'Leave him alone.' Not everyone can do that, but I think you boys can."

"What if other students won't listen?" asks Matt.

"You can always ask someone to help, like a teacher or other adult," you respond. "You can only do your best. But, like I said before, I think that others take their lead from the two of you. My guess is that people *will* stop if you say something."

"Yeah," says Jacob, "but suppose they just think we're lame? How many friends do you think we'll have then?"

You shrug. "If you decide to stand up for others, I guess that's the chance you'll have to take." You try some more flattery: "Listen, Jacob, I don't think anything you do will cause anyone to think you're lame. People respect you, and I believe that they'll listen and follow what you say and do."

That seems to mollify Jacob, and you move on. "I'm going to be talking to the whole class about this. I want everyone to be in the position to stop mean acts. But I wanted to talk to you first because you're leaders, and you can help everyone else."

Again, both boys silently nod.

"I'll be giving the whole class some opportunities to come up with things to say or do in those types of situations," you say. "But for now, do you have any questions?"

They shake their heads, and you all return to the building.

Back in your office, you become conscious that you haven't yet addressed the pejorative use of the word "gay," or the issue of who's vulnerable to teasing, or the idea that it's everyone's responsibility to stand up to not only teasing but also racism, sexism, and the other bad "isms." Now you feel the responsibility on *your* shoulders. You sigh and begin planning tomorrow's class.

SITUATION 15: THE LOSS

* * *

Soccer game

Woodrow Wilson Elementary School

Sedgewick, New Jersey

Asset 24—Bonding to school

Asset 30—Responsibility

It doesn't look good. The score is even at three, and there's less than a minute to go. You need a win to take the championship and send the home-crowd parents away happy, but the opposing Wildcats have the ball and are about to score.

Their player takes a shot, but your goalie blocks it! He throws it out to your best player, Mateo Gonzales. He dribbles the ball down the left sideline toward the goal.

"Bring it to the middle!" you yell, and Mateo tries to shift course. The two defenders beside him, however, box Mateo in.

"Pass it! Pass it!" you yell, without realizing that there's no one in position to pass to. The rest of your offensive team trail at least 10 yards behind the defenders. Now there's no time left to pass.

Mateo retains control of the ball, moves slightly toward the center, and kicks the ball toward the goal. However, the angle is too great for him. As the crowd cheers and then groans, the ball barely touches the outside of the goal and bounces out of bounds. The game ends in a tie; you've lost the championship.

Some of your boys are teary-eyed as you gather them around you. They can barely sound the compulsory cheer for the other team. Over on the sidelines, they collapse on the bench, heads down.

In the locker room, you emphasize to your team how proud you are of them, how close you came to the championship, and how they gave it their best.

Tim Lavine raises the first complaint. "Did you see all those fouls? We weren't getting any calls! It should have been 3-0, not 3-3!"

"It's not fair!" agrees Kiyoshi Osawa. "We deserved to win!"

A small voice comes from over your shoulder. "It's my fault," says Mateo. "I should have scored. It was an easy kick."

You wait to hear from the other players, the ones who should have been in position to receive the pass from Mateo, but nobody says anything.

Just then the principal enters the locker room. "Congratulations on a great season," he says. He turns to Mateo before leaving. "Almost, Mateo. That was a great try."

So it's settled: Mateo lost the game and the championship.

"Wait a second," you say to all your players. "Mateo did a great job just getting the ball close to shooting range. But he was covered and had no one to pass to. Where was the rest of my offense?"

"Hey, I was running as fast as I could," says Tim. "It's not my fault if he's past me. I would've been there in another second or two. He could have waited."

"No, he couldn't have," says someone else. "There wasn't any time left."

"There was enough time to wait and pass," says another voice. The discussion has degenerated into a blame game.

"That's enough," you shout, and everyone stops. "We all share in the blame as well as the credit. We're a team. We win together, and we lose together. That's the bottom line."

While the players get dressed and leave, you wonder if you've done enough. It's the end of the season, and you're not certain that they got the message.

Over the weekend, you stew about the situation, feeling helpless. What more can you do? You could talk with the players individually about the importance of accepting responsibility. Each player, you're certain, would listen and nod, but you doubt if the effects would be lasting. The next time the boys lose a game, one or two might own up to being responsible—especially if it's obvious. If one of them says, "It's my fault," then the others will feel let off the hook. Most will either explicitly say or implicitly believe that they were not to blame.

You try to remember how you took losses when *you* were a kid: did you accept your responsibility? You honestly can't recall any instances one way or the other. You tell yourself that if you were on a team now, you'd certainly take responsibility.

That's when you realize what you have to do.

YOU'RE THE COACH!

WHAT WOULD YOU DO?

Think about the situation as if you were there yourself, particularly in terms of the **bonding to school** and **responsibility** assets. **How would you communicate to your team that taking responsibility is nobler and more productive in the long run than affixing blame?** How would you handle the situation in a way that would promote assets and make a positive impact?

Monday morning you make your way to the main office, where you ask the principal if later you could have a few moments on the P.A. system. She says yes and you return to your office and chat with the secretary until the morning bell.

At 9:15, you return to the main office. You unfold your notes, sit by the microphone, and wait for the principal to introduce you. Then you say the following:

"I want to thank everyone for supporting us throughout this season. Each and every one of our players did an outstanding job, and the fact that we didn't win the championship should not diminish what they have accomplished this year.

"I know that people feel bad about our loss of the championship last Friday evening. Believe me, the players and I feel that loss more than anyone. We wish we could have won—but we didn't. The other team played the game a little better than we did, and they tied us in a fair contest.

"I want to say something about how the game ended. It ended when Mateo Gonzales missed a shot at the goal just as time ran out. That was too bad. But Mateo is in no way to blame for losing the game. He played exceptionally well, and if there had been more time on the clock, if there had been a teammate he could have passed to, if any of a thousand things had happened differently during the game, we would have won.

"In the locker room after the game, Mateo bravely took responsibility. I commend him for that; he's a fine athlete. But someone who should have taken responsibility didn't. Someone was more responsible than anyone else for the loss on Friday night, and that someone was silent.

"That someone, of course, is me. As the coach, I'm responsible for how my team plays. If I'd coached just a little better, if I'd emphasized one thing as opposed to another, if I'd made the right decisions on substitutions and strategies during the game, we would have won. I'm not saying that I'm to blame for the loss. I'm saying that I'm as much responsible as anyone else.

"What does that mean? It means that I'll remember this game, and next time—next year—I'll try not to make the same mistakes. I'll try to improve. I think we all will. But taking responsibility is the first step to improving. If I think only that I did a great job, then what reason do I have to become a better coach?

"So again, thank you for your support. I hope we can bring you a championship next year."

You put away your notes and return to your office.

You get a visitor during the first recess, and it's not whom you expect. It's not Mateo, thanking you for absolving him of all the responsibility. It's not Tim, apologizing for so readily affixing blame and shucking it off himself. Instead, it's Sally Cole, the older sister of Barry Cole, one of the players on the team.

"I wanted to tell you that Barry's better now," she says, standing in front of you. You motion for her to sit down, but she shakes her head.

"Better?" you ask. "What was the matter?"

"He was really down this weekend," she continues. "He blamed himself for the loss. He said he should have been in position to get a pass from Mateo. He wanted to tell everyone he was sorry, but he couldn't think of how to do it."

"I wish he would have talked to me."

Sally shrugs. "He didn't want to. But today, when he heard you over the P.A., I guess it made him feel better. He told me a little while ago that he was glad you said what you did."

"Because . . ."

"Because," says Sally, "now he doesn't feel as bad. You're the one who messed up, not him."

You nod, trying to figure out whether you should feel good or not.

"Well, thank you, Sally, for coming in to tell me that, and please tell Barry that he had a great season and has nothing to feel bad about."

"Sure." She spins on her heels and walks out.

You *think* that was a positive outcome, but maybe you shouldn't expect every single student to get the message instantaneously. In any case, you don't have time to worry about it. It's time to switch to basketball.

HUDDLE

INSTANT REPLAY

THE PROBLEM	THE ASSET-BUILDING SOLUTION
Your group of female players don't take their abilities seriously.	• Help build asset 16, high expectations. • Focus on their strengths during practice to show them what they're capable of doing.
You hear one student say to another, "You are so gay!"	• Help build asset 15, positive peer influence, and asset 26, caring. • Talk with a few students that peers look up to and ask them to be role models by sticking up for people when they hear hurtful comments.
Team members blame one player for a loss and don't accept their own responsibility.	• Help build asset 24, bonding to school, and asset 30, responsibility. • Model accepting responsibility by stating your own role in the loss.

Asset-Building Coach: *It's certainly not easy to change an entire culture, is it?*

Asset Referee: You're referring to your efforts with the girls in your sports camp?

ABC: *It's too much for one person to do. Here are kids—boys and girls—who have been acculturated for years to think that sports is still primarily for boys—despite all the changes Title IX has promoted. How much time do I have with them? A week? A couple of months? The odds are stacked against me.*

AR: And yet you made some progress.

ABC: *That's true, but it was still difficult.*

AR: That's also true.

ABC: *Listen, I have a thought regarding the way I helped coach the girls in that sports camp. I focused on their strengths—hitting, fielding, whatever. I increased their abilities in something they already did well. I didn't address their weaknesses until much later. That seems to be just the kind of strategy you'd use with young people in general.*

AR: That's right. You'd also want to conduct some assessment before, during, and after training. And you'd want to find some way to sustain the relationship as well as the asset building.

ABC: *So coaching young people in sports really isn't much different than coaching them in anything. If I apply the philosophy of focusing on strengths, then I'm probably going to be helping young people build assets.*

AR: Other things being equal, that's correct. Keep in mind that relationships are key and that many environments—peer, school, home, community—need to repeatedly and consistently reflect that philosophy. That changes the odds you mentioned before in your favor.

ABC: *But I don't have control over all those environments.*

AR: That's why it's important for as many people as possible to adopt the philosophy—to pass along the message that we need to focus on young people's strengths.

ABC: *Okay. So I should be a model for others.*

AR: It would be to your advantage in the long run. Think about the situation in which some children were teasing the boy, Coby. You recruited models, Matt and Jacob. In that situation, you use the power of peers to lead the way. Those two boys have a lot more influence over their classmates than you ever will. That goes for a multitude of situations, not just this one.

And think about other adults, too. The bias against females is insidious. It permeates our culture. In the sports world, that bias is probably more blatant than anywhere else. Talk with your colleagues. If your students' peers and families hold those biases, then you need as much help as you can get to tell those students the other side of the story.

ABC: *What about the loss? A soccer game is one thing. What if you lose the entire season? What if your team just isn't good enough to win anything?*

AR: What do you think?

ABC: *I think that to a certain extent, the same strategies apply. Share responsibility. Learn from mistakes. Do the best you can. Look to the future.*

AR: Okay . . .

ABC: *But it's tough! It's tough to look to the future when you know it's going to be the same as the past and the present.*

AR: Then maybe you need to redefine "winning."

ABC: *Winning is getting more points than the other team.*

AR: Sometimes. But other times winning is doing better than you did before. You may have to break down the elements of the game. You may have to say, "Pat, I want you to get a foot on the ball at least three times every possession. Lee, I want you to dribble for at least 10 consecutive seconds. Team, I want you to take at least 12 shots for the game." Work with what you have.

ABC: *That doesn't address the emotional part of the game for the kids.*

AR: Winning always beats losing, but young people can have fun even when they don't win. They can learn new skills. They can show teamwork and determination and a love of the game. Emphasize these aspects of playing with a team that has more losses than wins.

ABC: *Okay, I can accept that. What's next?*

AR: Our last situations center around performance. What does it mean to perform successfully? And what happens when you don't perform successfully?

SIXTH 6 PERIOD

PERFORMANCE

SITUATION 16: THE STUDENT-ATHLETE

* * *

Basketball pep rally

Forest Hill High School

Laudenburg, Kentucky

Asset 21—Achievement motivation

"I know y'all got a good team here, and I know you're gonna win tonight! But let me tell you somethin' important, and that's you gotta study hard. You gotta pass your tests, so you can go to college, and you gotta graduate college. Be as good as you can be. That's the way to succeed—doin' your best in school. Go get 'em, Falcons!"

The student body erupts, and the band starts playing the Falcons fight song. Meanwhile, you escort Manny Clete off the stage. "I really appreciate your coming here," you say as the two of you head to the parking lot. "It's not every day that the students get to hear from an all-star NBA guard at their pep rally. It meant a lot to them."

"Glad to be of service. They're a nice bunch of kids."

"I was just wondering. I know you were drafted out of your first year of college. What is it that you remember liking in school? Any particular subjects that you found especially interesting?"

Manny Clete looks at you briefly, then turns the corner of the building looking for his limo. "Uh, no, man, I can't think of . . . no, wait, chemistry. I liked chemistry." The limo pulls up, and he rushes toward it. At 6'9", his stride allows him to outpace you, and you struggle to keep up. "Why chemistry?" you ask.

Clete reaches the limo and opens the door to the back seat. He turns to you. "Look, man, I went to school to play ball. That's what I do. School was"—he glances at the driver and smiles—"a *vehicle* for me to play ball. It didn't matter what subject I took, okay? But I'm glad I went. School's important. Peace." He disappears into the car, and it speeds away.

The drums and the cheers get louder as you slowly walk back to the gym. You know that of about 500,000 high school basketball players in the country, only about 50 are drafted into the professional ranks. Most of those who are lucky enough to go pro last only a few years before returning to the real world of jobs and debts. You also know that basketball is big in this town: the games draw more people than any other civic event. And you know that, as head coach of the Forest Hill High School Falcons, the responsibility placed on you is greater—no exaggeration—than on anyone except the mayor, and even that's debatable.

Still . . . you glance down at your whistle as you reenter the gym; the cheerleaders are leading the student body in cheers. Are you thinking about them, the students? Are you thinking about what's best for them *beyond* high school?

You feel a hand on your shoulder; it's Principal Dent's.

"This is what it's all about," he says.

"They're good kids," you say.

"They're great kids," he says. "They're the best students in the state."

"Are they?" you ask. You think of your five starters. You doubt that any of them is carrying more than a 1.5, and Filkins probably isn't even doing that. "What do you mean?"

But now the cheering is too loud to carry on a conversation, and you let it drop.

YOU'RE THE COACH!

WHAT WOULD YOU DO?

Think about the situation as if you were there yourself, particularly in terms of the **achievement motivation** asset. **How would you support the "student" part of "student-athlete" without antagonizing your team, the principal, and the school community?** How would you handle the situation in a way that would promote assets and make a positive impact?

"Absolutely not!" says Principal Dent, straightening the papers on his desk. "It's a district decision."

"No, I checked into it," you say. "It's up to the discretion of the school."

"Even if it was—and I'm not positive you're correct on that—the answer is still absolutely not."

You figured that raising the minimum grade for athletic participation from a 1.5 to a 2.0 would be an uphill battle, and now you're thinking that maybe confronting Principal Dent wasn't the best way to start.

"The task isn't impossible. I believe in these kids, and I think they can all get 2.0's. With some tutoring, some mentoring . . ."

"You can tutor them 24 hours a day, but you can't guarantee me that they'll all make the grade. That means you can't guarantee me that they'll remain on the team, and that's not acceptable!"

"So you'd rather have a good basketball team than good students?"

Principal Dent stands up, and so do you. You're three inches taller than he is, and you figure you need all the help you can get.

"Listen," he says in a voice that's more menacing for its evenness. "Do not doubt my devotion to my students. I have been principal of this school for 14 years, and I was a teacher for 11 years before that. I've hired four basketball coaches, and I can hire a fifth. So you make your choice now: leave the minimum requirement at a 1.5 . . . or just leave."

Again, think about the situation. Have your actions made a difference? What would you do?

You can't win this—at least right now. "Think about it," you say, and walk out of the office.

But you're the one who has to think about it. Everything you stand for tells you that letting student-athletes slide by with a 1.5 average is doing them a disservice. But if you're fired, or you quit, then it's doubtful that anything can change.

You return to your office and throw yourself into your easy chair. You're angry at Principal Dent for being old-fashioned, you're angry at Manny Clete for being hypocritical, and you're angry at yourself for being powerless. You thumb through your players' records and you shake your head. You firmly believe that students should not be playing ball if they're not excelling in school.

Then it comes to you. Of course. You can't kick anyone off your team for having poor grades, but you certainly don't have to start them—or, for that matter, play them at all. That's a great way to motivate students' achievement.

Your coaching staff turns out to be both loyal and understanding. They help you draft new strategies based on who will comprise the new Falcon team. You're not sure they like it, but you challenge them to continue to win with the new personnel.

Following that, you and the coaches sit down with your players to explain the new expectations. The best students will start and get the majority of the playing time. You will monitor students' grades and be in regular contact with their teachers. When they do better then they'll be rewarded with more playing time.

"I don't get this, Coach," says Filkins, the one who stands to lose the most. "I thought the Falcons way was to win."

"You're right," you say. "The Falcons way *is* to win. But there are many ways to win. One is to field the best athletes and not worry about what happens to you after you leave this school. The other is to field the best *student*-athletes and prepare you for life after high school. For most of you, life is going to be much more than basketball."

"You'll be fired after we start losing," says Filkins, surprising you with his lack of tact.

"Maybe so," you say. "But you know what? I'd rather be fired knowing that I tried to make good students out of you than keep my job knowing that I didn't."

The next day Principal Dent calls you into his office. He remains sitting; you remain standing.

"What do they call that in football, an end run?" he says. He's not smiling.

Then he looks directly at you. "Don't lose."

"I can't," you say.

SITUATION 17: THE POOR PLAYER

* * *

Softball practice

Clearview High School

Clearview, Arizona

Asset 18—Youth programs

Asset 38—Self-esteem

You sigh as you watch yet another ball pass under Sharon's mitt. At shortstop, she's a little slow getting the glove down—just as she was a little slow reading the ball come off the bat when you had her in the outfield and a little slow going to her left when you had her at first base. She didn't want to catch, she couldn't pitch, and she has poor judgment in determining when to take an extra base. As a batter, she has difficulty driving the ball.

In short, despite your coaching—including as much one-on-one as you could afford—Sharon is not a good ballplayer. She's a great kid—eager to learn, generous with her teammates—but whoever suggested that she play softball was doing her a disservice.

That person may have been Sharon's mother. The opening home game of the season is still two weeks away, yet her mother already e-mailed you to inform you that Sharon's relatives from Tucson will be at the game en masse. You e-mailed back to say that you had yet to evaluate the players and to make up the starting lineup, so it wasn't clear how much playing time Sharon would actually get. But your attempt at kindness and subtlety backfired. Sharon's mother replied that however much time Sharon got in the field and however many times she got to bat would be just fine with her grandparents, aunt, uncle, and three cousins.

You recognize, of course, that the twin goals of winning and giving everyone playing time are often contradictory, but in the past you've had the luxury of covering for inadequate players or else cutting them from the team. This year the situation is different. Your starters are good, but your bench is weak. And the new school policy is not to cut anyone from the team.

Sharon herself adds to your predicament. She's a nice girl with a delicate ego. Sharon genuinely enjoys playing softball, so you'd hate to see her languish on the bench the whole season while everyone else is playing. On the other hand, you don't want to play her and put her in the position of being blamed for a team loss. Becoming unpopular with her teammates wouldn't do Sharon's self-esteem much good.

You need to do something in the next few days because all the players—starters and bench—need to know where they stand. Bench players should know that they'll get into games in certain situations, but what can you tell Sharon: "Sharon, you'll get into any game in which we're either 10 runs ahead or 10 runs behind"?

YOU'RE THE COACH!

WHAT WOULD YOU DO?

Think about the situation as if you were there yourself, particularly in terms of the **youth programs** and **self-esteem** assets. **How would you meet the needs of both Sharon and your team?** How would you handle the situation in a way that would promote assets and make a positive impact?

You have several individual meetings with students in your office over the next week or two; you consider the one with Sharon very important.

You begin your talk with her by asking her to share her strengths with you.

Sharon smiles shyly. "Well, I try hard. I listen to you. I try to pick up my teammates. But if you mean in terms of hitting, or catching, or running, well then, I don't know. I guess I don't have many strengths there."

"Pick something."

"I don't understand. Pick something?"

"Sharon, I want to play you. I want you to be in a game where your entire family can cheer for you. But I need to find the right place for you to help the team. So I want you to pick one aspect of softball and concentrate on that one thing. It could be bunting, or ground balls, or base running. Choose something, and I'll help you work at it. We'll set some goals, and when you meet them, I'll be able to put you in games in specific situations. And I'll know that I can count on you."

"So you're saying that you can't count on me now."

At that moment, you wish that you weren't a coach. You wish that you were a chemist off in some lab somewhere busy with beakers of bubbling liquid rather than an influential adult staring into Sharon's disheartened face.

But you *are* a coach, and Sharon deserves the truth.

"As you said, Sharon, I can count on you to try hard, to listen to me, and to pick up your teammates. But right now I can't count on you to field a ball cleanly, to run the bases wisely, or to hit effectively. You need more practice, and I will help you get that practice, only we'll focus on one or two areas instead of a dozen."

Sharon nods and grimaces, then begins to tear up, but suddenly her face hardens as if she's resolved to succeed in something difficult yet inevitable.

"Okay. I'll practice bunting. That way you can put me in situations that call for moving runners ahead. And you won't have to worry about me messing up in the field."

She gets up to leave.

"Sharon, wait." Now it's your turn to resolve to do something difficult yet inevitable.

"I know that your family plans to attend the opening game. I won't start you, but I'll put you in at first base for at least a few innings."

Sharon smiles. "Thanks, Coach. That's nice of you. I won't let you down."

She leaves your office, and you resume your balancing act: the players' feelings, the team's record, the student body's expectations, your need to reward performance, and your desire to motivate young people.

It's all part of the job.

SITUATION 18: THE GIRL WHO COULDN'T SEE HER FUTURE

* * *

Physical education class

Tree-on-the-Knoll Elementary School

Crawford, North Carolina

Asset 40—Positive view of personal future

The question was simple: "What do you want to be when you grow up?" And the answers were to be expected: Air Force pilot, scientist, teacher, major league baseball player, doctor, someone who works for charities, president, and even one writer. It was one question out of a 10-question "Fun Survey" you give out midyear. Some of the other questions included: "What's your idea of a great vacation?" "Who's your favorite character in a book or movie?" "If you could speak a language that you don't speak now, which one would it be?" "What's one thing you would change about this school?"

De'Shonda answered every question except "What do you want to be when you grow up?" She didn't run out of time—it wasn't the last question. Maybe she couldn't make up her mind, you think. Or maybe she got sidetracked and forgot that question.

But neither of those explanations fits De'Shonda's personality. She's a thoughtful, decisive, even stubborn girl. She's persistent and not easily distracted. You remember her behavior early in the year when everyone was practicing foul shots. Most of the students—boys as well as girls—were content to shoot 3 or 4 out of 10. But De'Shonda practiced even when others were taking recess, until she could shoot at least 5 out of 10. You also remember her initial difficulty keeping her balance on the beam. You lost count of the times she fell off, but she got right back on every time until she could stay up as long as she wanted.

So it's not likely that De'Shonda couldn't make up her mind or simply forgot the question. Maybe, you think, she felt that writing something down would somehow commit her to that course, and she didn't want to be bound by it. In any case, you like De'Shonda's spirit, and so you call her in for a chat.

You offer her a package of cheese and crackers as you sit with her on the couch in your office.

"I notice that you didn't answer the 'What do you want to be when you grow up?' question on the Fun Survey," you begin.

De'Shonda chews and nods.

You raise your eyebrows and shake your head. "Any reason?"

She swallows. "It's not important."

This, you think, is one of those conversations in which you have to take the lead or else it'll last the entire day.

"Answering the question isn't important? What you want to be when you grow up isn't important?"

"Both."

"De'Shonda, I don't quite understand. Could you tell me about it?"

De'Shonda swallows. "Could I have some water, please?"

You give her a bottle from the refrigerator, which she thanks you for and takes a gulp from.

"I just don't think I'm going to be anything when I grow up. I mean, I guess I'll maybe get married and have a bunch of kids. But that's it."

"Why?"

"Why?"

"Why do you guess that's it? You can be anything you want. You can be an astronaut, a senator, a physician"—you smile—"a coach even."

De'Shonda smiles back. She stands up. "Right. Hey, Coach, I gotta get going. Thanks for the crackers."

You watch her leave and you realize that something is very wrong. You know that De'Shonda comes from a poor family, that she has seven brothers and sisters, and that her father left her mother when De'Shonda was two. You know that the family has had several encounters with the police, most involving one or another of the mother's boyfriends who have lived in the house over the years.

But De'Shonda is resilient. She appears to be a happy girl. She's at least an average student, and you've been impressed with the way she carries herself and interacts with others: she's tough without being aggressive, friendly but not a joiner. You like her a lot, and you want to help her.

YOU'RE THE COACH!

WHAT WOULD YOU DO?

Think about the situation as if you were there yourself, particularly in terms of the **positive view of personal future** asset. **How would you help De'Shonda to be more positive about her future? Is it harmful to raise her expectations when she's not prepared to follow through with them?** How would you handle the situation in a way that would promote assets and make a positive impact?

A week later, De'Shonda is again sitting on your couch, eating cheese and crackers.

"Coach, why are you so good to me?" she smiles.

"I'm a sucker for kids who shoot fouls."

"You still want to know what I want to be when I grow up?"

"I want to know why you don't think it's important."

De'Shonda sighs. "You just don't know how it is. I'm poor, my family's messed up, I'm not a great athlete, I'm not a great student.

I'm just—I'm just who I am. I know it's your job to get me to feel good about myself and stuff like that, but I don't think you want me to tell you, 'Oh, sure, Coach, I'm going to be President of the United States,' when I don't believe it."

"Have you ever heard of John Johnson?"

"Who? John Johnson? No."

"Bear with me for a minute. John Johnson was born in Arkansas. His grandparents were slaves. His mother got as far as the third grade. John attended the Arkansas City Colored School."

"Arkansas City Colored School? Hey, what year was this?"

"This was in the 1920s and 1930s."

"Oh, okay. I was wondering how they could have that."

"Things were different then, much harder for folks who weren't white. Anyway, the Arkansas City Colored School went up to only the eighth grade. So John's mother worked extra jobs to raise enough money to take her and John to Chicago. The father stayed behind."

"Why are you telling me this, Coach?"

"Here's a kid. He's African-American. He's poor. He's got this really strong Arkansas accent in the big city of Chicago. Now what would you say his chances are for making something of himself?"

"Not good."

"You're right, his chances were bad, but have you ever heard of *Ebony* magazine?"

"*Ebony?* Sure."

"John Johnson started *Ebony.*"

"No way."

"Yes way. Look, you can read about John Johnson if you want. You can read about Bill Clinton, whose mother left him to live with his grandparents when he was only two years old. You can read about George Shearing, who became a famous jazz pianist even though he was born blind. Or about Jim Abbott, who became a major league baseball pitcher despite having no right hand. The point is, many people have overcome terrible situations to make wonderful achievements."

De'Shonda sighs.

"What would you like to be when you grow up, if you could be anything?" you ask her.

She smiles. "You're gonna laugh."

"Maybe. Tell me, anyway."

"An engineer."

"An engineer? Like a civil engineer?"

"I don't know what that is. No, Coach, like a train engineer. I'd like to be an engineer on a train."

"And?"

"And what?"

"And what do you have to do to become an engineer on a train?"

"I don't know. Do well in school, I guess. Study. Stay out of trouble."

You take De'Shonda's hands and look directly into her eyes. "De'Shonda, listen to me. You are a very capable girl. I'm not just saying that; I really believe in you. You have amazing persistence. Look at how you kept practicing those foul shots until you could shoot them better than anyone. Look at how long you practiced on the beam until you could stay up there longer than anyone. De'Shonda, you have talent and the will to succeed. If you study and stay out of trouble, I think you can be whatever you want to be, including a train engineer."

De'Shonda looks down. You're not sure she believes you, but you think she at least doesn't *dis*believe you.

"Thanks, Coach," she says, and gets up to leave. "Anything else?" she asks.

You shake your head. "Nope, I think that's enough for now."

"What'd you say the name of that guy was who started *Ebony?*"

"John Johnson."

"John Johnson. Yeah." She smiles suddenly. "Did you coach him, too?"

Now it's your turn to smile. "No, he was a year or two before my time."

"Yeah, I guess so. But I bet someone like you coached him. See you, Coach."

De'Shonda is out the door before you can say, "Thank you."

LOCKER ROOM

INSTANT REPLAY

THE PROBLEM	THE ASSET-BUILDING SOLUTION
A visiting professional athlete reminds you that the "student" part of student-athlete is often forgotten.	• Help build asset 21, achievement motivation. • Talk with the principal about grade standards for student-athletes. Make good grades and high marks important to your players.
A mom wants to see her not-so-talented player in the season home opener.	• Help build asset 18, youth programs, and asset 38, self-esteem. • Focus practice on one or two specific areas of play for that student.
One of your players doesn't have plans for her future.	• Help build asset 40, positive view of personal future. • Provide examples of successful role models who succeeded despite adversity. Offer encouragement.

Asset-Building Coach: *Those were difficult situations. I was up against so much.*

Asset Referee: Yes.

ABC: *The endings won't always be nice, though. Principals fire coaches who challenge them. Coaches make kids feel bad. And some students don't see much of a future for themselves.*

AR: Yes, all those things do happen.

ABC: *But what I did worked—or seemed to.*

AR: That's true. But we have certain limitations in this book. These situations are typical but not exclusive. Think of them as 'core.' From these core situations spring an infinite number of similar yet distinct situations. In some of those, the coach does get fired. In others, the coach resigns. In still others, the coach's arguments sway the principal. Each distinct situation has an infinite number of factors that interact and form an infinite number of possible combinations.

ABC: *I understand that. I was only wondering if maybe my solutions were a little too pat.*

AR: The intent of this book is to give you experience and practice, not to depress you. Would you like to encounter a situation in which you fail miserably?

ABC: *No, no, not at all. I was speaking, uh, rhetorically.*

AR: Comments?

ABC: *Well, the situation with Sharon was the most difficult of all. I'm in the position of having to hurt someone who can ill-afford getting hurt. She's on the team, but she can't play well. There's no easy answer to that one.*

AR: You're absolutely right.

ABC: *That's what I was afraid of.*

AR: Don't worry about what you can't do as much as what you can. Sharon has responsibilities, too. She has a responsibility to do as well as she can and to balance what she really wants with what she thinks other people want.

ABC: *It doesn't make it easier.*

AR: No, it doesn't.

ABC: *I have a question about De'Shonda, the girl who didn't think she would amount to much. I think I may even know the answer, but I'll ask anyway. I showed her some role models and talked with her, but how do I know if that built assets or made a positive impact? I've felt that way in several other situations, too. How do I know I succeeded?*

AR: You said that you thought you knew the answer.

ABC: *I'm thinking that the answer is I have to wait and see.*

AR: That's part of the answer, but there's a little more to it than that. This isn't just 'show.' Positive impact is made because of a continuing relationship of trust and support. Even if De'Shonda doesn't strive to do better, she'll know that you care about her, especially if you continue to monitor her behavior and offer your help. The knowledge that you care may be more important than your ability to help her resolve any one issue. These situations are short segments of a continuum. The extent to which adults make positive impacts on young people is determined by their performance all along that continuum.

ABC: *I have a question about this whistle, too. Does it work?*

AR: Does it work? Of course it works. Consider how many times you looked at it and were reminded that coaching is about the players, not the coach.

ABC: *No, I mean, does it work when you blow it? I never blew it. I almost blew the whistle once or twice, but for some reason I didn't.*

AR: Whistles can be useful devices for getting attention, but too often they're wielded as symbols of authority. Maybe you didn't blow the whistle because you don't have a strong need to exercise authority over your players.

ABC: *So it does work . . . as a whistle?*

AR: If you want to try it, you can. Suffice it to say that if "IT'S ABOUT THEM" reminds you to care about the young people you're coaching, then the whistle works. In the meantime, you've completed this part of your training.

ABC: *I have? Great! Wait. This part?*

AR: The rest of your training will continue as you work with and relate to your own students. Good coaches—like good athletes—train continuously.

ABC: *And I did well—in this part of the training?*

AR: You did very well. Your strengths are in your desire to do well by your players and your ability to see things from their perspective and let go of your own need to make decisions for them.

ABC: *Thank you.*

AR: At the beginning of this book I asked why you became a coach. I thought that a typical response would be, "I like sports, I like teaching, and I like kids." Now I suggest that you reflect on that question and add something to your answer, such as: "I'd like to make a positive difference in the lives of the young people I come into contact with as a coach." The impact of making that difference, that's the important thing.

Now you resume coaching, perhaps with more knowledge about why you're doing what you do. I wish you the best of luck, and I thank you for participating in these situations. When you promote Developmental Assets with young people, and when you keep in mind that "IT'S ABOUT THEM," that's when you're coaching at your best.

EQUIPMENT

40 Ways Coaches Can Build Assets for and with Youth

The original 40 Developmental Assets are research based and copyrighted. But many communities and groups find it inspiring and thought-provoking to adapt the framework for specific purposes. Here is one group's interpretation of the assets for coaches.

Support

1. **Family support**—Have a team meeting with athletes and their families prior to the season to outline expectations and guidelines.
2. **Positive family communication**—Remind parents to use positive encouragement and constructive criticism.
3. **Other adult relationships**—Assign a player (not their own child) for parents to watch during the game and at the end to tell the player something he or she did well.
4. **Caring neighborhood**—Remind players to invite people to the games.
5. **Caring team climate**—Encourage team members to cheer for each other.
6. **Parent involvement with team**—Encourage parents to be involved as assistant coaches, treat providers, etc.

Empowerment

7. **Community values youth**—Have the players thank the team sponsor.
8. **Youth as resources**—Ask players for input on how games are going and what they need to improve on.
9. **Service to others**—Have players pick up trash around the dugout and field after the game.
10. **Safety**—Never jeopardize the physical health of a young person.

Boundaries and Expectations

11. **Family boundaries**—Keep in mind that family commitments are important and come before sports.
12. **Team boundaries**—Ensure that the team has clear rules and consequences.
13. **Neighborhood boundaries**—Be respectful at the field, behaving in the neighborhood as you would want people to act in yours.
14. **Adult role models**—Your behavior sets the standard for athletes and spectators.
15. **Positive peer influence**—Practice and promote unselfishness and teamwork.
16. **High expectations**—Have realistic expectations and maximize your athletes' potentials.

Constructive Use of Time

17. **Creative activities**—Create a team cheer.
18. **Youth programs**—Teach age-appropriate skills. Encourage effort without focusing on results.
19. **Religious community**—Don't schedule practices to conflict with religious commitments.
20. **Time at home**—Encourage players to practice at home.

(continues)

40 Ways Coaches Can Build Assets for and with Youth *(continued)*

Commitment to Learning

21. **Achievement motivation**—Make sure athletes tell you what their goals are and praise them as they move toward meeting their goals.

22. **Team engagement**—Encourage players to watch the game even when they are on the bench.

23. **Homework**—Encourage players to get their homework done before their team commitments.

24. **Bonding to team**—Remember, it's still a game; fun needs to be everywhere.

25. **Reading for pleasure**—Have a book about an inspirational athlete to give to an MVP after each game. Have players write something that they learned in the book.

Positive Values

26. **Caring**—Praise players with a smile, nod, or compliment. Remember they look to you for approval.

27. **Equality and social justice**—Don't play favorites; move players around to different positions. Aim for active participation from every player.

28. **Integrity**—Treat players with respect, avoiding put-downs, sarcasm, or ridicule, and require the same from them.

29. **Honesty**—When you tell a player what you like about her or his effort or performance, be specific.

30. **Responsibility**—Give players responsibility such as helping with equipment.

31. **Restraint**—Focus on good sportsmanship. Stay calm when players make mistakes.

Social Competencies

32. **Planning and decision making**—Be organized and ready for practices and games.

33. **Interpersonal competence**—Model for athletes the need to encourage players as they improve their skills.

34. **Cultural competence**—Make sure players who are new to the sport understand its rules and strategies.

35. **Resistance skills**—Remember that young people involved in positive organized activities are much less likely to be involved in risky behaviors.

36. **Peaceful conflict resolution**—Demonstrate how to peacefully resolve conflicts during games. Set the standard for absolutely no swearing.

Positive Identity

37. **Personal power**—Involve players in making decisions by asking them for input and inviting their questions.

38. **Self-esteem**—Help players develop confidence and self-esteem by greeting them individually when they arrive.

39. **Sense of purpose**—Praise players for the important role they play in the team (i.e., team leader, biggest fan) or for a particular skill they have mastered.

40. **Positive view of personal future**—Remember that you are developing good human beings first, developing athletes second.

Asset-Building Ideas for Coaches

Coaches teach young people not only the rules and strategy of games but also important lessons about life. You can help young people develop confidence and self-esteem, help them learn to resolve conflicts peacefully, teach them ways to take care of their health and well-being, and help them develop skills for communicating with others. Here are a few ways coaches can be asset builders.

Learn the names of all the players on your team and call them by name. Make a point to talk at least once with each player each time you practice or play.

Create and maintain a positive atmosphere. Two top reasons young people participate in sports are to have fun and spend time with their friends.[1] Winning is not one of their top reasons.

Focus on helping players get better, not be the best. It will reduce players' fear of failure and give them permission to try new things and stretch their skills.

Know that highly competitive sports can often cause a great deal of stress for young people. The intense pressure that goes along with trying to be the best can sometimes lead to unhealthy outcomes such as substance abuse and/or eating disorders. Be careful not to push young people too hard and learn about the warning signs of possible problems.

Care about your athletes' lives outside of the sport and show them that they are valuable people as well as team members.

Adapt your teaching style and language to the players' age level. Young children do not always know sport terms. Use words and concepts they understand. On the other hand, older youth may be more successful when they understand the big picture of what they are trying to accomplish as well as the specific skills or strategies needed.

Set goals both for individuals and for the team. Include young people in setting these goals.

Catch kids doing things right. Be quick to praise a player's efforts. The best feedback is immediate and positive.

[1] "Factors Underlying Enjoyment of Youth Sports: Sport and Age Group Comparisons" by Leonard W. Wankel and Philip S. J. Kreisel. *Journal of Sport Psychology,* March 1985, 51–63.

(continues)

Asset-Building Ideas for Coaches *(continued)*

Use the sandwich method of correcting a player's mistake. First praise, then constructively criticize, then praise again.

Always preserve players' dignity. Sarcasm does not work well with young people. They may not always remember what you say, but they always remember how you said it.

Insist that all team members treat one another with respect. Then model, monitor, and encourage respect. Have a zero-tolerance policy for teasing that hurts someone's feelings.

Be specific about a code of conduct and expectations for athletes, parents, spectators, and team personnel.

Encourage athletes to do well in school and to be motivated to achieve.

Respect other activities and priorities in athletes' lives. Avoid conflicts with their other commitments and respect their need for time with their families.

Find ways each child can participate, even if he or she is not particularly skilled in the sport.

Listen to and encourage your athletes' dreams, concerns, and desires—sports-related or otherwise.

Develop leadership skills in young athletes by giving them opportunities to lead practice drills and develop a team code of conduct.

Take time at the end of practice to have the group offer positive comments about each player's performance that day. Make sure no one is left out.

Split up cliques on the team by mixing up groups for drills and scrimmages.

Plan a community service project for the team. It teaches players to give something back to the community.

If you have an end-of-season gathering, take time to say a few positive things about each player. Avoid Most Valuable Player awards and other "rankings." Focus on the relationships, the improvement of the team, and the unique contributions of each player.

The Truth about Steroids

What exactly are steroids?

Anabolic steroids are drugs that come from the male hormone testosterone. They promote muscle growth and increase lean body mass. Anabolic steroids are approved for many medical uses; however, they are abused by some athletes and others hoping to improve performance and physical appearance. These nonmedical uses are illegal and carry many health risks.

Myth: A lot of people take steroids.

Fact: Only about 2 percent of students in 8th, 10th and 12th grades have ever used steroids.

Myth: Only males take steroids.

Fact: Males account for more steroid use than females, but women and girls do take steroids. Girls make up about one-third of those who take steroids in high school. The main reason for their use is to lose fat and gain lean muscle.

Myth: Compared to other drugs steroids have few negative effects.

Fact: Steroids have many physical and emotional side effects.

Physical effects for males:
Shrunken testicles
Reduced sperm count
Impotence
Baldness
Breast development
Painful urination

Physical effects for females:
Facial hair growth
Change or cessation in menstrual cycle
Enlargement of clitoris
Deeper voice
Smaller breasts

Physical effects for adolescents:
Stunted growth

Physical effects for all:
High blood pressure
Liver tumors
Jaundice (yellowish coloring of skin)

Emotional effects for all:
Wide mood swings
Uncontrolled anger and aggressiveness
Depression (upon stopping use)
Paranoid jealousy
Extreme irritability
Delusions
Impaired judgment stemming from feelings of invincibility

Resources

ORGANIZATIONS

National Alliance for Youth Sports
2050 Vista Parkway
West Palm Beach, FL 33411
800-688-KIDS or 800-729-2057
www.nays.org

Positive Coaching Alliance
Stanford University
Department of Athletics
Stanford, CA 94305-6150
650-725-0024
www.positivecoach.org

COACHING RESOURCES

The Double-Goal Coach: Positive Coaching Tools for Honoring the Game and Developing Winners in Sports and Life by Jim Thompson. Published by HarperResource. The tools included in this resource are based on Jim Thompson's Positive Coaching Alliance. These strategies reflect the "best practices" of elite coaches and the latest research in sports psychology.

Phil Jackson on Positive Coaching. In this 40-minute VHS tape, basketball coach Phil Jackson talks about his history as both coach and player and how he has used positive coaching techniques with his own players. Available at www.positivecoach.org.

Positive Coaching: Building Character through Sports by Jim Thompson. Published by Warde Publishing, Inc. This 400-page book is filled with ideas and information for coaches who want their young athletes to truly enjoy their sports experience.

DEVELOPMENTAL ASSETS RESOURCES

The Asset Approach. A great handout for sharing the power of assets with parents, this eight-page booklet introduces adults to the power of using the developmental assets in their daily interactions with young people. (Also available in Spanish.)

"You Have the Power" sports posters. A set of eight posters that inspire kids in K–12 with positive asset-based messages about sportsmanship and life. These posters help readers of *Hey, Coach!* put into practice the positive coaching ideas from the book.

In Our Own Words. This set of eight posters—one for each asset category—features phrases and words that 17 young people used to describe what those categories of development mean to them. Great for locker rooms.

Me@My Best: Ideas for Staying True to Yourself—Every Day. This 16-page booklet introduces developmental assets to youth and inspires them to find and build upon their own strengths. Use it to support the young players you work with. It's also a great piece for youth to read and work on with an adult partner.

Take It to the Next Level: Making Your Life What You Want It to Be. In this 20-page booklet, young people focus on their successes and explore what they really want and how to get it through activities and journal topics based on the developmental assets. Another great tool to share with your players.

You Can. Inspire young players in the locker room with this colorful, eye-catching poster. *You Can* highlights the eight asset categories, explaining in one short sentence the meaning of each.

Assets and Coaching Situations

This chart shows which assets are promoted in the situations in this book. Keep in mind that other assets may in fact be promoted, depending on the specific circumstances of each situation.

EXTERNAL ASSETS	SITUATION	PAGE
Support		
1. Family support		
2. Positive family communication		
3. Other adult relationships	5	36
4. Caring neighborhood	7	47
5. Caring school climate	6	40
6. Parent involvement in schooling	6	40
Empowerment		
7. Community values youth	7	47
8. Youth as resources	1	17
9. Service to others		
10. Safety	9	53
Boundaries and Expectations		
11. Family boundaries	8	50
12. School boundaries	Warm-up	11
13. Neighborhood boundaries	5	36
14. Adult role models	4	33
15. Positive peer influence	14	78
16. High expectations	13	75
Constructive Use of Time		
17. Creative activities	2	21
18. Youth programs	17	95
19. Religious community		
20. Time at home		

(continues)

Grade Levels and Coaching Situations

This chart shows which grade levels (or corresponding ages) are featured in the situations in this book. Keep in mind that virtually all of the situations can be generalized to other grade levels.

GRADE LEVEL	SITUATION	PAGE
Elementary school	Warm-up	11
	5	36
	12	67
	14	78
	15	82
	18	98
Middle/junior high school	2	21
	6	40
	7	47
	9	53
	13	75
High school	1	17
	3	25
	4	33
	8	50
	10	59
	11	63
	16	91
	17	95

Sports and Coaching Situations

This chart shows which sports are featured in the situations in this book. Keep in mind that virtually all of the situations can be generalized to other sports.

SPORT	SITUATION	PAGE
Baseball/Softball	11 17	63 95
Basketball	4 10 16	33 59 91
Football	1	17
Gymnastics	6	40
P.E. Class or Multisport	Warm-up 13 14 18	11 75 78 98
Soccer	5 15	36 82
Swimming	8	50
Tennis	9	53
Track & Field	7	47
Volleyball	2 12	21 67
Wrestling	3	25